Cyber Nation:

How Venture Capital & Startups Are
Protecting America from Cyber
Criminals, Threats and Cyber Attacks.

ROSS BLANKENSHIP
Venture Capital, Cybersecurity Expert
& CEO, AngelKings.com

THANK YOU

Thank you to my family, always all-embracing and supportive of my father, The Blessings, and brother Michael. It is important for me to quantify how to pursue my dreams by giving back [...]

Thank you to the brilliant cybersecurity advisors who worked with me at Angel Kings' funds to pursue this JKM solution [...]

Thank you to Brian Kushy, whose book became a native focus a great inspiration for our book on cybersecurity.

Thank you to the brilliant venture capital and angel investors at AngelKings.com

*To learn about Angel Kings and one of our cybersecurity venture capital funds, visit AngelKingsvc.com today.

CONTENTS

PREFACE

Cybercrime is the greatest threat to our nation's economy. For example, Lloyd's and the *University of Cambridge Centre for Risk Studies* estimate that a cyber attack on our nation's power system, alone, could cost up to $1 trillion.[1] This real threat comes from China, Russia, North Korea and many other foreign governments. Cybercrime is both a private enterprise and a nation-sponsored threat. In America, hackers are launching cyber attacks against banks, stealing private information and selling your private data on open exchanges and forums hosted through anonymous networks like "Tor." New forms of cyber terrorism continue to create deep paralysis and heighten our fear that our privacy is being violated. This fear is now a reality. We must act now to prevent further breaches in our nation's economic infrastructure.

In fact, just as I was writing this book on cybersecurity and the impact on America's economy, the Office of Personnel Management (OPM), the branch of the Federal Government that maintains employee data and policies, reported an attack that affected nearly 20 million

---

[1] See the report at: The Emerging Risk Report, lloyds.com, The Centre for Risk Studies at the University of Cambridge, 2015.

people.[2] That's everyone who's ever worked in the American government, submitted a background check, or taken a polygraph to get secret clearance. There's never been a bigger wake-up call to start improving our nation's cybersecurity defenses.

Whether it is the electrical grid that binds cities together, the Wi-Fi networks and cellular towers, or the Internet of things (IoT) in your home, attackers are on the move, usurping privacy and stealing your money. If we idly sit as these cyber attacks continue, businesses and consumers will lose faith and our economy will suffer. Scared money does not make money; unless we act with haste, power and a sense of purpose, American consumers will stop spending as much of their income and companies will lose.

When I founded Angel Kings (AngelKings.com), a venture capital fund whose mission is to solve real problems by investing in the best startups, I began with cybersecurity.

However, I never knew how big of a threat cybercrime was until two things happened in my life:

---

[2] https://www.opm.gov/cybersecurity/

First, while in law school, I worked briefly at the U.S. Securities and Exchange Commission (SEC). During my time in the SEC's enforcement division, we encountered a new phenomenon, and growing cybercrime, law firms and companies' email systems were now being "phished" for inside trading. These cyber criminals were sending "phishing emails" to employees, associates and senior partners at law firms. Once the victim at the firm clicked these baited-link emails, the cyber hacker would receive access to every deal, transaction, and pending merger or acquisition. We discovered that cyber hackers at this level were beyond sophisticated. I saw first-hand how much a cyber attack could impact the public markets: many of these cyber phishing attacks took less than an hour, but created profits in the millions of dollars, and disrupted deal flow in some of the biggest mergers and acquisitions.

Second, I've seen the simple, but devastating side of cyber attacks. I have founded several e-commerce websites, invested in a portfolio of companies as an early investor, and relied on these websites to make profit; however, I've been attacked at every level by what's called a Distributed Denial of Service (DDoS attack). Although most of our sites are now protected using sophisticated cyber software, at the time, we had no relief. These attacks consisted of a "botnet" of zombie computers unknowingly sending traffic and ping requests to websites. The only "knowing" participant was the cyber hacker in his basement.

Our Chief Information Officer (CIO) was confident that a competitor had hired an offshore DDoS hacker, who must have used a botnet to inflict weeks of cyber attacks on our primary website, it was hard to prove and more costly to litigate. Indeed, unlike the attacks we saw at the SEC, these attacks were brute, unsophisticated, and seemingly impossible to defend. The good news: whether you're a major corporation, new startup, or consumer looking to protect yourself, you no longer have to pray for relief. You can do something now to prevent yourself from falling victim to the economic pain and mental angst that a cyber attack causes.

The cybersecurity industry is booming. Our experts at Angel Kings predict that the cybersecurity industry will grow to become more than $150 billion by 2020. As long as hacking – both sophisticated and brute – is remains profitable, high-margin and continues to grow exponentially, cyber attacks will happen. These attacks can cripple our government, damage our nation's economy, and paralyze our population.

As we become increasingly dependent on technology – in our homes, in our businesses, and our government – the *new World War* is cyber terrorism.

Cyber Nation is an introduction on the world of cybersecurity, the threats we face, the hackers who continue to cripple our economy, and how we can fight back. The fundamental premise is this: we can, and must, use the economics of cyber attacks to win the war against cyber terrorism.

I hope this book on cybersecurity gives you enough information to get know the key players, to be inspired to work in cybersecurity, and to invest in the hottest sector of our nation's economy. There is no reason you shouldn't make money, while fighting the next World war.

I am a free-market thinker, a venture capitalist and early investor in some of the most remarkable companies in cybersecurity at our company, Angel Kings. Most importantly, I am an American who believes we have a moral and social responsibility to protect our nation's freedom.

I'll show you how venture capital and startups are empowering and protecting us from the nation's next great threat. And if you're inspired too, **join us at** AngelKings.com.

1

CYBER CRIMINALS: WHO, WHAT, WHERE, WHEN, & HOW THEY ATTACK

"The art of war is of vital importance to the State. It is a matter of life and death, a road either to safety or to ruin. Hence it is a subject of inquiry which can on no account be neglected."

Sun Tzu, *The Art of War*

WHO ARE THE CYBER CRIMINALS?

The media might have you believe that all cyber criminals are part of organized rings in far places such as China and Russia, but hackers and identity thieves exist everywhere and make up every demographic. From high school students who entice fellow students to send nude pictures, then blackmail those students, to a man who was charged with counterfeiting money orders to pay for items he found on Craigslist, cyber criminals are presenting a growing collection of crimes.

On the lower level, cybercrimes perpetrated are fraud, blackmail, or misuse of computer networks by one individual. Monetary values associated with the crimes can range from a few hundred dollars to many millions of dollars.

On a higher level, cybercrimes are part of global integrated organized crime groups. These groups use cybercrimes within their communities as a way to fund activities or outwit legal resources. Organized cybercrime often takes place through underground markets, where cyber criminals barter illegally obtained identities and information.

Cyber criminals do not discriminate. They are attacking our government and the people within. Driven by ego, money, and the prospect of fame, they attack because they can, because we allow them to and because we neither protect ourselves, nor disclose when we are attacked.

As we become increasingly dependent on technology, we allow ourselves to be attacked with little defense. The criminals listed below are only part of the problem. Corporations should begin to identify weaknesses and vulnerabilities in their networks, and address attacks when they happen, not months later. But be careful, that cyber criminal might just be your next door neighbor hacking alone in his or her basement. Cyber criminals make-up all races and religions.

THE MOST WANTED CYBER CRIMINALS

To get an idea of these cyber criminals, you can scroll through the FBI's "most-wanted cyber criminals" list. You'll find criminals involved in racketeering, conspiracy to commit bank or computer fraud, identity theft. These cyber criminals are considered so dangerous that the FBI has offered millions of dollars in reward money for information leading to their capture. To view a full list of the FBI's most wanted cyber criminals, visit: *https://www.fbi.gov/wanted*

Here are examples of some of the most notorious cyber criminals, still on the run…

EVGENIY MILHAILOVICH BOGACHEV **(RUSSIA)**

Bogachev tops the FBI's list and warrants a $3 million reward. Bogachev's crimes include conspiracy charges, racketeering, violation of the Computer Fraud and Abuse Act, bank fraud, money laundering, wire fraud, aggravated identity theft, and computer fraud. Bogachev created a racketeering enterprise that installed Zeus software on individual and business computers without authorization from the computer owner. The malicious software was used to steal data, including passwords, logins, and bank account numbers. The information was sold on the underground market or used to login to bank accounts and steal funds.

PETERIS SAHUROVS **(RUSSIA & UKRAINE)**

According to the FBI, "Peteris Sahurovs is wanted for his alleged involvement in an international cybercrime scheme that took place from February of 2010 to September of 2010. The scheme utilized a computer virus that involved the online sale of fraudulent computer security programs that defrauded Internet users of more than $2 million." Sahurovs' scheme of using fake software to steal from naïve computer users, continues to this day.

Viet Quoc Nguyen (VIETNAM)

 Wanted by the FBI for hacking into email service providers, Nguyen stole confidential information contained in emails. The email providers were all US-based, and Nguyen got away with billions of email addresses contained in proprietary marketing information for some email users. In addition to the email schemes, Nguyen generated a revenue stream by hacking networks and redirecting Internet traffic to websites.

OTHER MOST WANTED CYBER CRIMINALS:

NICOLAE POPESCU (ROMANIA)

According to the FBI, "Nicolae Popescu is wanted for his alleged participation in a sophisticated Internet Fraud scheme where criminal enterprise conspirators, based in Romania and elsewhere in Europe, posted advertisements on Internet auction market sites for merchandise for sale. Such advertisements contained images and descriptions of vehicles and other items for sale, but those items did not really exist."

ALEXSEY BELAN (RUSSIA)

According to the FBI, "[b]etween January of 2012, and April of 2013, Alexsey Belan is alleged to have intruded the computer networks of three major United States-based e-commerce companies in Nevada and California. He is alleged to have stolen their user databases, which he then exported and made readily accessible on his server. Belan allegedly stole the user data and the encrypted passwords of millions of accounts and then negotiated the sales of the databases."

Sun Kailiang (CHINA)

According to the FBI, "On May 1, 2014, a grand jury in the Western District of Pennsylvania indicted five members of the People's Liberation Army (PLA) of the People's Republic of China (PRC) for 31 criminal counts, including: conspiring to commit computer fraud; accessing a computer without authorization for the purpose of commercial advantage and private financial gain; damaging computers through the transmission of code and commands; aggravated identity theft; economic espionage; and theft of trade secrets."

The common thread between the above criminals is, (i) how crippling and widespread their attacks were on American consumers and enterprises – in each instance costing millions, and even billions, in economic damage; (ii) that these cyber attacks also went undetected for days, weeks and even months before being detected; and (iii) that each criminal is protected by the state or nation in which they reside. Like Osama bin Laden, these cyber terrorists are living in plain sight of governments and people who turn a blind eye toward their terrorist actions. Later in *Cyber*

Nation, I'll discuss private and government solutions to fight back and penalize these countries for condoning attacks. For now though, these cyber criminals are still on the run, unless we do something drastic now.

HOW CAN WE STOP THE FBI'S MOST WANTED CYBER CRIMINALS AND CYBER ATTACKS?

The only way we're going to capture these cyber criminals is by using a **three-part approach** that blends both offensive and defensive measures from our Government, private enterprises, including the best cybersecurity startups.

1. CROWDSOURCE INVESTIGATIONS -

We should release every internet record and file we have on these suspected cyber criminals. This data includes IP addresses used, names of friends and family, all usernames used, previous addresses, bank and financial records. Make every cyber attack transparent; let the world know, and the affected population, who is responsible. I liken this crowd sourced approach to how a cold-case was solved using the popular internet forum, Reddit. While some might argue these cyber criminals deserve due process, these are terrorists and shouldn't be protected under the Geneva Convention. The American government should also work with crowd sourced platforms like BugCrowd and Synack whose platforms have enough white hackers to back-trace cyber attacks and these cyber criminals.

2. PENALIZE – WITH 3X THE POWER

Penalize every company that knowingly allows malicious traffic or turns a blind eye to these cyber criminals who host illicit forums and networks. After notifying the Internet Service Provider (ISP) that their servers have been used by cyber terrorists, give them reasonable notice and then 30 days to block these cyber criminals. Some would argue that *First Amendment* principles prohibit taking down cyber criminal forums; some would argue that it's not the company's responsibility to monitor what goes on, but the reality is that we're talking about cyber terrorists and a new World War that will require heightened awareness and actions by all.

Penalize every nation that knowingly harbors cyber fugitives. Later in the book, I discuss economic sanctions, but the idea is to levy massive economic warfare on any nation who is responsible, directly or indirectly, for allowing a cyber attack. The country should feel three-times the amount of economic impact that any American company or federal governmental agency felt.

3. SLOW THE FLOW OF TRAFFIC

Just as we try to block illegal drug-traffickers from crossing our borders, we need to slow inbound traffic coming from the states that are sponsoring cyber attackers. Though many cyber attackers use localized ISP providers based in America, there's still volumes of traffic coming from European and Asian countries. Some would argue this approach isn't fair for either legitimate web commerce or for the companies who rely on these countries for business, but the financial impact on our industries at large outweighs this "fairness." The state of cybersecurity is so dire that we have to act now or billions more in damages will be realized.

***

It's **important to note** that the U.S. government could incentivize the private sector to direct this traffic. After all, penalizing everything isn't always the best solution. I'm not arguing we need a "cyber-police" – in fact, as a free-market economist, I believe the private sector could accomplish most of the goals above. As an example, cybersecurity startups like Cloudflare allow ISPs and individual domains to block traffic from certain countries.

THE GROWING POPULATION OF CYBER CRIMINALS

While the most-wanted list and high-profile cyber attacks that make media headlines — such as the hacks of retailer networks that impacted Target and Home Depot in 2014 — are often the types of criminals and crimes we think of when we consider cybercrime, the reality is that you don't even hear about the majority of these crimes.

Most cybercrime does not make the news because it's not high profile. In many cases, no one even realizes a crime is being committed until much later. And the population of cyber criminals is growing because it's often looked at as a low-risk proposition for anyone willing to make money by dealing in shady areas. It's difficult to crack down on cybercrimes because the Internet makes it increasingly easy for criminals to target others in an anonymous and remote manner. Cyber criminals even hack into computers for the purpose of using those computers to conduct other hacks and crimes — in this way, the criminals create a buffer between themselves and law enforcement.

CYBER CRIMINALS BY THE NUMBERS

According to Bloomberg, 33 percent of cyber attacks originate in the China, but cyber criminals come from all over the globe.[3] Statistics indicate that 41 percent of the world's attack traffic comes from China.

The top ten nations for cyber criminal activity include:

1.	China	41% (of the world's attack traffic)
2.	United States	10%
3.	Turkey	4.7%
4.	Russia	4.3%
5.	Taiwan	3.7%
6.	Brazil	3.3%
7.	Romania	2.8%
8.	India	2.3%
9.	Italy	1.6%
10.	Hungary	1.4%

---

[3] Milian, Mark. "One-Third of Cyber Attack Traffic Originates in China, Akamai Says." *Bloomberg.com*. Bloomberg, 23 Jan. 2013. Web. 01 July 2015.

China, Russia, and Turkey are the countries with the most foreign cybercriminals. China, however, remains the home origin of nearly 33% of cyber attacks.

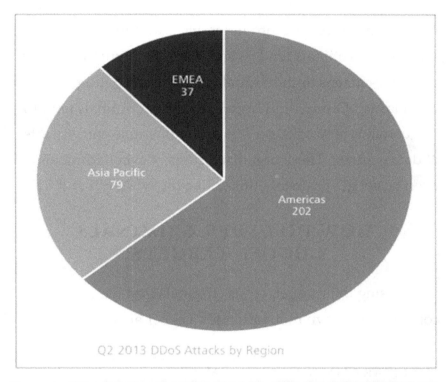

Figure 1: *"The Americas, and the U.S. specifically, saw the most DDoS attacks in Q2, and enterprise services are proving to be the most vulnerable, with e-commerce coming in at a close second."*[4]

---

[4] Lunden, Ingrid. "Akamai: Half of All Internet Connections Now At 4Mbps+, Safari Remains Most Used Mobile Browser." *TechCrunch*. TechCrunch, 16 Oct. 2013. Web. 03 July 2015.

WHEN AND WHERE DO CYBER CRIMINALS ATTACK?

Individual cyber criminals tend to target areas of opportunity, which means they look for vulnerabilities in a network or process or for vulnerable individuals. This is why cyber criminals tend to target at-risk populations, such as senior citizens or individuals who are struggling monetarily. Groups and organized cyber criminals tend to target major networks, servers and vulnerable entry points at data centers. These organized rings of cyber criminals even target government entities like the NSA, FBI and CIA.

HOW DO CYBER CRIMINALS CHOOSE TARGETS?

In choosing their target, cyber criminals first have to consider their own motivation for a cyber attack.

MONETARY GAIN & PROFIT MOTIVE

The biggest motivation for cybercrimes is monetary gain. Cyber criminals choose targets that match their own capabilities, offer a point of entry or vulnerability, and are most likely to pay off. Cybercrime is profitable, easy and quick money. Cyber criminals with sophisticated capabilities or the network to offload large amounts of credit card or other data are likely to target banks, retail networks, and financial businesses, all of which offer bulk access to personal data to anyone that can breach the network. The value of a U.S. credit card number, along with matching Social Security number and date of birth, is about $25. That's not enough value to cyber criminals looking to sell the data unless they can access a network with hundreds or thousands of credit card numbers and related information.

THE POLITICS OF CYBERCRIME

When politics, either domestic or international, is the driving force behind a cyber attack, criminals choose a website or organization that espouses or supports an opposing political, cultural or religious viewpoint. Most of the time, the attack is not about money or specific gain, but about defacing, embarrassing, or raising awareness. Individuals are not often targets of these attacks, though corporate entities and government agencies are. You will even see state-sponsored attacks by countries such as China, who in 2015 attacked the Office of Personnel Management – hacking millions of federal government employees' private and personal data.[5]

---

[5] https://www.opm.gov/cybersecurity/

EGO & NARCISSISM

Cyber criminals spreading cyber terror for the sake of their egos often develop wide-reaching malware that attacks computer systems or networks. In many cases, the malware never generates a revenue stream for the attacker, but he or she enjoys the "fame" that comes with launching a widespread attack. Not unlike serial killers who have sociopathic tendencies, these cyber criminals get an adrenaline rush from watching themselves on the news and hearing about destruction they've caused.

Individual cyber criminals or those with less access to underground networks usually target people instead of organizations. Instead of selling the data obtained, the criminal may use personal information to make purchases or access funds and benefits directly. In these cases, criminals conduct phishing schemes, attempt to hack passwords, use email and social media to coerce information from people, or even go through garbage or old files for useful information. When a single cyber criminal gets hold of enough personal information to commit identity theft, they may be able to access thousands of dollars in goods before the identity theft is realized and the victim takes steps to close accounts and freeze assets.

COMMON CYBERCRIME "BUSINESS MODELS":

(1) Buy and sell stolen information in online marketplaces
Stealing credit card data and personal information is lucrative for cybercriminals because it provides direct and easy gains in the underground marketplace. Prices for a customer's personal information can range from $8 to $45, underscoring the low-risk high-reward nature of cyber crime.

(2) Crime-as-a-service
In the underground markets, organizations and individuals can buy or sell exploit kits, botnets, denial of service attacks, or just their skills. Services can run from $1 for 1,000 CAPTCHA-breakings to $350 to $450 for consulting services such as botnet setup.

(3) Attracting capital "investors"
Skilled individuals will always be in demand in the eyes of organizations — namely, organized crime syndicates — that seek to make a profit. In some cases, individuals are coerced or recruited by these organizations for the purpose of leveraging their talents.

(4) Market their supplies and services like a business
"Suppliers" of data in this underground market economy today operate "businesses" that may involve everything from marketing themselves online via Twitter to providing bulk discounts, free trials, and customer support for customers (criminals who purchase this stolen data).

A Snapshot Of Market Prices For Credit Card Data: April 2014
The Cybercriminal's Prize: Your Customer Data And Competitive Advantage

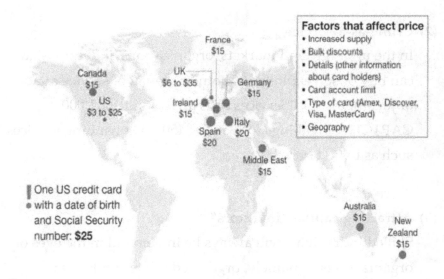

6

---

6 Shey, Heidi, and Kelley Mak. "Forrester." *Research: Research : The Cybercriminal's Prize: Your Customer Data and Competitive Advantage* . N.p., 6 Aug. 2014. Web. 01 July 2015.

THE BIGGEST CYBER THREATS

Larger cybercriminal organizations are also targeting certain industries. In recent years, the biggest threats were to organizations within the retail and banking industries. In the future, I believe immediate threats will migrate to healthcare and insurance, defense, and the Internet of things.

Healthcare and insurance networks are at risk in part because of the enormous amount of identifying data they contain. A patient's administrative and clinical medical records contain more than enough information for identity theft—these records include full names, dates of birth, social security numbers, addresses, and telephone numbers. Often, healthcare networks even contain information about credit card and bank accounts because patients allow this information to be put on file for payment of co-pays and deductibles.

The healthcare industry does work diligently to protect data by maintaining compliance with laws such as the Health Insurance Portability and Accountability Act (HIPAA). These laws govern how data must be stored, secured, used, and transmitted in a healthcare environment. However, as clinical staff move increasingly toward interconnectivity and mobile device use — things that are improving patient experiences and the efficiency at which treatments and clinical functions occur — they make themselves more vulnerable to hacks. There are great startups like TrueVault that are building protection for healthcare data in the cloud. However, one company can't solve the problem of protecting healthcare data.

A concern for the Healthcare industry is that hacks and cybercrimes aren't just going to target patient data that allow criminals steal identities or access bank and credit accounts. Some cyber criminals are using data — or selling it to others to use — in order to access healthcare benefits. By pretending to be someone else, individuals are gaining access to treatments in emergency rooms, clinics, and hospitals — often leaving the victim on the hook for any bills. Even when no bill is generated, the victim could lose out on healthcare benefits or have to fight for them because the insurance company believes it has already paid for the service.

As more and more hospital machinery and equipment is being developed with Internet or wireless capabilities, the opportunity for dangerous healthcare cyber vandalism or terror attacks exists. Conceivably, cyber criminals could harm specific or random patients by hacking into devices meant to disburse medications or perform procedures. Finally, research labs are also connected, which means cyber criminals can steal or vandalize important proprietary data about research and development (R&D). The impact is increased costs and time as research processes are disrupted, and cyber criminals can sell the ideas and data on the black market to be used by others — often in an inappropriate or dangerous manner.

Another growing threat in cybersecurity is defense, particularly for the United States. The U.S. Defense Department invests in new technology such as drones or automated defense measures. The nation also relies on power grids and other infrastructures that have become highly automated and interconnected, all of which leaves the country vulnerable to cyber warfare.

While defense is a national concern, attacks via the Internet can also impact the security of your home. With more individuals relying on home automation, cyber criminals are gaining increasing access to functions such as home security, home climate control, and home electronics. These services and devices are supposed to keep you and your home safe;

while they do provide added security, they also open you up to other vulnerabilities.

A great example of new vulnerabilities in the home is with Google's Nest Lab thermostats, smoke detectors and "Dropcams." Connected through the Wi-Fi in millions of American homes, these devices can be de-encrypted and attacked with simple password hacks. Just imagine how devastating this attack could be: what if your baby was sleeping and being watched by a stranger who hacked into your Dropcam? This actually happened and is likely to happen again as millions of homes adopt this technology.

It's absolutely critical that companies like Google identify these cyber threats and notify consumers of the potential dangers of installing "internet of things" hardware. These notices should come standard in the instruction manuals of every new IoT hardware for the home.

WHERE ARE THE 3 BIGGEST, MOST IMMEDIATE THREATS FROM CYBERCRIME?

HEALTHCARE & INSURANCE

- Hardware and robotics account for a significant increase in hospital care/surgical devices.
- Doctors and nurses are sharing important patient data via mobile and cloud. HIPAA at risk.
- Research labs for pharmaceutical companies are also increasingly cloud-based.
- Patient information being falsely used for procuring health insurance.
- Biggest threats: patient privacy, patient safety with drug development, hardware malfunctioning with medical devices, and insurance industry theft.

DEFENSE

- American defense (large cap) spending is increasingly spent on hardware such as drones and space-based defense/offense measures.
- Major energy, financial grids and networks are subject to attacks by foreign entities.
- Police and law enforcement is now cloud-based with new sharing that could be hacked.
- Biggest threats: operational protection of markets, hardware/drone operations, police/safety.

INTERNET OF THINGS

- Millions of homes projected to be connected to Internet of Things ("IoT") by 2020.
- Major corporations like Google, General Electric, Cisco, and Honeywell will need to ensure all Wi-Fi devices and internet based software/hardware hybrid protects are protected.
- Access to consumer homes bring inherent and growing risks for safety and privacy.
- Biggest threats: Wi-Fi devices, hardware such as thermostats and smoke detectors, routers and internet-connected devices

WHAT STARTUPS NEED TO BUILD FOR THESE INDUSTRIES

Healthcare industry

On the hardware side: startups need to build protection for new hospital hardware and robotics. We must protect the core hardware in hospitals – EKG machines, heart monitors, pacemakers, oxygen respirators, and surgical robotics systems. This means providing secure blockers to protect against access from unidentified hackers. These hackers could easily interfere with the existing robotics. As robotics in surgical operations continue to increase, the threats will rise.

Additionally, there are opportunities in protecting hospital networks and security cloud systems for the largest hospital chains in the world including the U.S. Veterans Affairs (VA Hospitals), HCA, Inc., Ascension Health, Community Health Systems, NY Presbyterian, Catholic Healthcare West, Tenet Healthcare, Kaiser Foundation, the Cleveland Clinic and even regional chains such as The University of Pittsburgh, and MedStar Health at Georgetown Hospital.

On the cloud and software side, every time a patient's data is uploaded on Electronic Medical Records (EMR) like General Electric's Centricity, athenahealth, or Allscripts systems, there's a risk that the patient's data could be hacked. Even with the HIPAA rules, internal security like 256-bit SSL logins, and internal security, cyber threats exist against patient data. It's absolutely critical that we start doing something now so that nothing like what happened with the OPM and Federal Government, happens with patient data. We'll discuss Anthem Insurance's breach next.

Insurance industry

Insurance companies store more patient data than individual hospitals. With the added fact that insurance companies have begun merging and consolidating with the Affordable Care Act, or commonly known as Obamacare, there's a real need to protect these behemoths from attack. Large insurance companies like UnitedHealth, Kaiser, Anthem, Cigna and Humana, need to do a better job distributing patient data, securing records in the cloud, and ensuring their own employees aren't vulnerable to cyber phishing attacks.

When Anthem Inc. was attacked in 2015, immediately more than 80 million patient data was at risk. That's equivalent to nearly one in five Americans.

Whether selling to large enterprise companies like UnitedHealth, Kaiser and Anthem, or to smaller insurance companies and consultants, the Insurance industry is ripe for disruption.

Defense industry

On the hardware side: we see the biggest threats from cyber attacks being drone, space technology and military robotics. In each of these three, there's ample opportunity for startups to protect the remote access capabilities of hackers, to ensure that our satellites are protected, and our on-the-ground defenses cannot be interfered with.

On the drone front: as remote operated drones carry-on more attacks abroad in countries like Syria, Pakistan, Iraq and Yemen, we've got to make sure that these drones aren't susceptible to cyber-takeover. Drones like the *RQ-1 and MQ-1 Predators* can carry serious Hellfire missiles, Stingers, and Griffin air-to-surface weaponry. If one cyber-attack disrupted just one of the hundreds of monthly operative drones, an entire city could be attacked – killing thousands of civilians.

On the space and satellite front: increasingly our nation's defense rests in arms of thousands of satellites that orbit around the Earth. Protected by the U.S. Air Force Space Command, the U.S. Army Space and Missile Defense Command (SMDC) and monitored by the Central Intelligence Agency (CIA) and National Security Agency (NSA), these satellites are crucial to our national defense. In a *60 Minutes Report* by David Martin in April 2015[7], we saw first-hand how Chinese anti-satellite weapons could literally dismantle these satellites within an instant. According to General John Hyten, doing so could disrupt our nation's ability to communicate with troops, collect intelligence and fly drones.

Because satellites, defense and military spending is in the hundreds of billions of dollars every year, we can't think of a greater opportunity than this for cybersecurity startups.

The "Internet of Things" industry

---

[7] http://www.cbsnews.com/news/rare-look-at-space-command-satellite-defense-60-minutes/

The biggest threat from the rise of the Internet of Things – will be devices installed in homes such as Google's Nest thermostats, smoke detectors, cameras, from the unsecure routers and Wi-Fi networks, and lastly, remote security systems controlled by mobile devices.

Google must protect the constant data and monitoring taking place in the cloud through these devices. But consumers shouldn't expect anything more than standard protecting from this company. After all, Google has a history of monetizing personal and private data. Startups who are willing to build on-top of these new devices could benefit substantially.

With the Internet of Things have come popular security systems like SimpliSafe, ADT, and Google's Dropcam systems. In each hardware device, there's a new vulnerability. According to a report by Forbes writer Kashmir Hill, researchers Colby Moore and Patrick Wardle of Synack, discovered serious vulnerabilities on the Dropcam device. With the click of a button on the back of the Dropcam, "(the) attacker could install spyware to turn the surveillance camera into one that surveils audio and video of its owners, or install a program that could make them see video of the attackers' choosing."[8]

Dropcam, Nest, and security systems like ADT are just the start of the rise in new home technologies – there will be more systems built, and we'll continue to rely more on remote devices to bring comfort to our homes.

We cannot allow these vulnerabilities to continue. Consumers should be put on notice and companies must act fast before releasing new hardware for the home.

***

Startups and investors should look at these four industries: healthcare, insurance, defense, and the Internet of Things, as opportunities to build great products to protect America from cyber attacks. Each present ample opportunity for making money, while protecting the American consumers from malicious cyber attacks.

---

[8] http://www.forbes.com/sites/kashmirhill/2014/07/23/how-your-security-system-could-be-used-to-spy-on-you/

HOW CYBER CRIMINALS ATTACK

Cybercrimes occur in a variety of ways, and the methods deployed by cyber criminals depend on the reason for the attack and the person or entity being attacked. Common methods include hacking, distribution of malware, phishing, social media schemes, purchasing insider information, and stealing physical data.

COMPUTER AND NETWORK HACKS

Computer and network hacks are used in large-scale cybercrimes because it is much easier for smaller scale criminals to defraud an individual through malware or phishing schemes. In cases such as the Target breach, which compromised data for up to 110 million customers, hackers accessed the network by stealing credentials from a vendor contracted by the retailer. They used the stolen credentials to work their way into the network to a vulnerability point, which allowed them to steal the information without detection.

Hacking usually involves some form of stolen or compromised data or a network that is protected by weak security measures. While most organizations — those that deal with financial data — encourage strong password protocols, experts are increasingly stating that passwords are no longer enough to keep hackers at bay. As fast as encryption and password protocols are emerging, cyber criminals are evolving methods to get past those security measures. Most organizations are attempting to counter this with multi-stage authentication that includes measures such as device verification, biometrics, or information verification.

MALWARE

Malware is often the tool used to prepare for a hack, but it can also be used to scrape valuable information such as credit card numbers or passwords from networks, databases, and user computers. Malware is often some sort of software that is downloaded on a computer or network. A user downloads malware without meaning to when downloading free or low-cost software. Cyber criminals create such software as bait to trick people into downloading malware, but malware can also be attached to email downloads and other files, which is how cyber criminals distribute the software so quickly across hundreds or thousands of users.

PHISHING & HACKING SCHEMES

During phishing schemes, cyber criminals trick individuals into giving up information such as account numbers or login credentials. Phishing schemes might include:

- Fake phone calls from an entity claiming you owe money and asking that you schedule a payment by providing credit card or account information.
- Phone calls alleging that you have won a prize or are owed money, but you have to provide financial information to claim it.
- Spoofed emails that look like they come from your bank or financial institution about an issue, with a false link asking for your login information.
- Spoofed emails that look like they come from a legitimate business alleging that you owe money and asking for payment arrangements

- Emails offering assistance of a financial nature with links to sites that require your personal information.

Phishing schemes target the vulnerable. If someone is in financial duress or has filled out a form for financial assistance online, they may be targeted with phishing schemes offering too-good-to-be-true loans, for example. Senior citizens are often targeted with fear-mongering phishing schemes that play on a perceived ignorance about technology or other matters, and small business owners may be targeted with schemes that use common small-business fears and worries against the business owner.

SOCIAL MEDIA SCHEMES

Cyber criminals are rampant on social media. Some spoof real accounts and then use those accounts and the trust relationships associated with them to steal ideas and information. Others use the fact that people will download videos and pictures from friends on social media much faster than they might download email attachments; cyber criminals attach malware to these downloads, and they can spread to thousands of users in days or even hours.

INSIDER INFORMATION AND TRADING

When planning a cyber attack on a large organization, cyber criminals find insiders who are willing to provide or sell information. The information provided is often related to network security or login credentials, although the insider may even steal or help the outside criminal steal large amounts of data about the business, its employees, or its clients. The insiders also target law firms and publicly traded companies to trade insider information on the public markets. The U.S. Securities and Exchange Commission (SEC) needs to start notifying law firms and publicly traded companies that their systems are vulnerable to attack.

PHYSICAL DATA THEFT

Insider information is a form of physical data theft, but cyber criminals also steal physical data from individuals in a number of ways. One known scheme is for wait staff in restaurants to steal credit card information when patrons pay with a credit card. Data theft also occurs when individuals take information from documents that were not shredded or otherwise destroyed upon disposal.

CYBERCRIMES AFFECT EVERYONE

By understanding who cyber criminals are, when and where they attack, and how they attack, individuals and organizations can reduce their vulnerabilities. How can you better protect your company, home and individual data from cyber criminals?

- Being vigilant about your data and checking your accounts on a regular basis.
- Using strong data security protocols.
- Knowing that if something sounds too good to be true, it probably is.
- Limiting downloads and using services such as Dropbox to share files when possible.
- Being careful on social media and not downloading random files.
- Using technology and products provided by emerging companies to protect yourself against cybercrimes on computers, cloud networks, and mobile devices.

2

CASE STUDIES OF THE
BIGGEST CYBER ATTACKS

"One hundred percent of third parties showed
signs of compromise or indicators of threats...
Our global cyber landscape is a scary place."

-Chris Coleman,
Security Analyst with Lookingglass

In its Global State of Information Security Survey Report, PricewaterhouseCoopers (PWC) notes that the number of security incidents increased by 48 percent from 2013 to 2014, even though global security spending remained stalled with only about 3.8 percent of technical budgets allocated to security spending. [9]

In the past few years, signs of compromise and threats have turned into nightmare cyber attacks for several government agencies and public companies, including the Internal Revenue Service (IRS), Healthcare.gov, Target, Anthem, and Sony. These cyber attacks, which cost billions and impacted

---

[9] "Global State of Information Security Survey: 2015 Results by Industry." *PwC.* N.p., 30 Sept. 2014. Web. 01 July 2015.

millions of individuals, are currently some of the biggest cases of cyber attacks in history — and experts are warning that even bigger attacks could be looming. By studying the biggest cybersecurity fails of the past few years, though, organizations may be able to learn more about how cyber criminals operate and how networks can be protected.

THE MULTI-PRONG IRS DATA BREACH

Of all agencies that use your personal information, the IRS is probably secure, right? While the federal tax agency may protect taxpayer data with numerous security measures, it does make information available through a number of online services. Individual taxpayers can access their own data through several agency services, and organizations such as mortgage providers can access certain records with a few pieces of information and a signed release from the taxpayer.

Each of the access points or services provides a possible entry point for cyber criminals or hackers. In 2015, cyber criminals breached the IRS' network and stole tax refunds from taxpayers.

Hackers gained access to taxpayer information via an IRS-provided service known as *Get Transcript*. The service was built so that legitimate taxpayers can access copies of past tax returns when needed. To do so, you need four data points: Your filing status, address, date of birth, and social security number. The hackers attempted to access records through Get Transcript by entering information as many as 200,000 times; a bit over 100,000 of those attempts were successful, resulting in the compromise of that many taxpayer records.[10]

The breaches occurred between February and May 2015. The cyber criminals then used the information obtained through Get Transcript to file fraudulent tax returns. According to the IRS, the hackers got away with around $50 million in fraudulent tax returns.

Hackers continue to use social security, date of birth, and address information from another organization and cycled through various filing statuses in an attempt to find the right combination for access.

In Senate hearings on the subject of the IRS data breach, J. Russell George, the IRS' Treasury Inspector General, reported that his agency reviews the IRS every year to

---

[10] Phillips, Kelly. "IRS Says Identity Thieves Accessed Tax Transcripts For More Than 100,000 Taxpayers." *Forbes*. Forbes Magazine, 26 May 2015. Web. 01 July 2015.

determine how secure the agency is. George reported that the IRS continually failed to make recommended updates to its systems following these audits, and that 44 recommendations had not been acted upon by March 2015. Of those, ten recommendations had been made three years prior. Reports are that the IRS failed to act in part because security funding had declined in recent years; cybersecurity budgets for the agency totaled $187 million in 2011 and had dropped to $149 in 2015.[11]

Lessons from the IRS data breach include:

- Diminishing security budgets can put organizations at risk.
- Failure to act on known security vulnerabilities opens the door wider for cybercriminals.
- Hackers are getting increasingly sophisticated with their attacks, even accessing organizations in ways that appear legitimate to computer and security systems.
- Never centralize data onto one cluster of servers. Spread data and confidential information across clusters which are protected by both hardware and software defenses.

---

[11] Rein, Lisa. "IRS Failed to Address Computer Security Weaknesses, Making Attack on 104,000 Taxpayers More Likely, Watchdog Says." *Washington Post*. The Washington Post, 2 June 2015. Web. 03 July 2015.

HEALTHCARE.GOV'S CONSTANT BATTLE WITH CYBER CRIMINALS

As early as 2013, cyber criminals were targeting Healthcare.gov, the website used to access the federal health insurance marketplace. The Department of Homeland Security reported in 2013 that the website had come under more than a dozen attacks, though official reports at the time were that the attacks failed.

Healthcare.gov was targeted by cyber hacks that attempted to breach the network and access information. There were also reports that the site may have been targeted with what is known as a DDoS attack. DDoS, or distributed denial-of-service attacks, are created to make a system or site unavailable to users who are trying to access it.

While reports in 2013 were that none of the attempted hacks worked, the White House did confirm an attack in early fall 2014. At that time, the administration reported that a security breach occurred, but that it was on a test server and did not compromise the data for any individuals within the system. The breach may not have resulted in specific data loss, but it did raise some serious concerns about the security of the federal website. Healthcare.gov has a history of security concerns. Politicians, pundits, and security experts accused the administrators of the website of rushing to meet launch deadlines before the October 1, 2014 enrollment launch. According to reports, the website was initially launched before security testing was complete, and the site was not even up to federal standards.

Investigation showed that the test server intrusion that occurred in fall 2014 was possible because of security weaknesses on the site. First, the test server was connected to the Internet in the first place, which is not usually protocol with test servers. Second, the test server's password was still set at the default manufacturer setting, making it easy for hackers to guess using common password hacking programs or methods. Finally, the test server was not made part of regular security scans, which would likely have caught the first two issues.[12]

Within a month of the test server attack, Healthcare.gov did pass an audit from the Department of Health and Human Services Department. The auditors attempted to hack the site

[12] Pear, Robert, and Nicole Perlroth. "Hackers Breach Security of HealthCare.gov." *The New York Times*. The New York Times, 04 Sept. 2014. Web. 01 July 2015.

themselves and found that it held up well to cyber attack efforts. The auditors did note some security weaknesses that it recommended be addressed, including the site's failure to enforce rules about strong password creation. However, the fact that the IRS could be attacked at all, drives continued concerns for the need to protect the American people from cyber attacks.

Lessons from Healthcare.gov's ongoing battle with cyber attacks include:

- A cyber attack doesn't have to be successful to damage an organization by negatively impacting consumer trust as well as organizational reputation and branding.
- A rush to market can increase the chance that products or sites are vulnerable to attacks.
- Ongoing diligence is required, as cyber criminals are tenacious.
- We should increase our cyber defenses when there is data from 1,000 people or more. We should also de-centralize this data and store private data on servers that are externally hacker-proof.
- Our government should also be more careful picking cybersecurity vendors. The Federal Government likely spent more than $100 million

on this website,[13] but should have at least spent $10 million to test it for cyber attacks and hackers.

[13] http://www.washingtonpost.com/blogs/fact-checker/wp/2013/10/24/how-much-did-healthcare-gov-cost/

TARGET'S 2013 HOLIDAY DATA BREACH

In what seems like the stone that sent the retail cybersecurity wall crashing down, Target announced a major data breach following the 2013 holiday shopping season. At a time when more customers were in the store than any other time of year, cyber criminals gained access to the retailer's network and began syphoning credit card data off of the system. Because of the manner in which the hackers gained access, their activity went undetected for almost a month.

Over 100 million individuals were exposed in the attack. Target reported that the information compromised in the attack included mailing addresses, names, email address, phone numbers, and credit and debit card account data. According to the retailer, not all records compromised contained all those types of data; the most valuable data to these cyber hackers was credit and debt account numbers. They stole this data.   Law-enforcement officials also noted that names, phone numbers, and email addresses were stolen too; this added information provided cyber criminals with the information required to hack other consumer accounts or launch phishing schemes. Further, the credit card data breached in the attack included account numbers,

CVV security codes, and expiration dates. Could it have been a worse case scenario for Target?

ATTACK

The Target data breach was a result of hackers gaining undetected access to the network with credentials stolen from a refrigeration and HVAC company that does work for a number of Target locations.

Hackers gained access to as many as 110 million customer names, card numbers, expiration dates, and CVV security codes of the cards issued by financial institutions.

IMPACT

At least 90 lawsuits were brought against Target in the aftermath of the breach. All told, Target could face a $90 fine for each cardholder's data compromised, which translates to the $3.6 billion liability.

Profits fell nearly 50% in that fiscal quarter. Target's share price fell 11% during the same time.

Like the IRS breach, the hackers in the Target attack used legitimate credentials to initially enter the system. They began with stolen credentials from an HVAC company that acts as a contractor to several Target locations. From that entry point, the hackers were able to exploit a previously unknown flaw in what was then traditional retailer point-of-sale encryption. Payment Card Industry data requirements do mandate that any organization gathering credit and debit card information for the purpose of charging the card encrypt that information according to a sophisticated set of security rules. The cyber hackers, however, got into the system at a point in the process that let them scrape the data prior to some of the encryption processes.

Investigations into the breach indicate that Target was made aware of the breach by its cybersecurity service. According to reports, the retailer had time to act to stop the theft of data, but it failed to act in a timely manner to prevent the theft. Because of Target's slow movement on the issue, it is facing dozens of lawsuits and up to $3.6 billion in fines.[14] In the early summer of 2015, Target attempted to settle the lawsuits with $10,000 for each account holder impacted by

---

[14] Williams, Alex. "Target May Be Liable for Up To $3.6 Billion From Credit Card Data Breach." *TechCrunch*. N.p., 23 Dec. 2013. Web. 01 July 2015.

the breach, but that settlement was held up in court at the time.

Lessons from the Target breach and following actions include:

- A lesson on paying attention to security reports and warnings from security services that you employ.
- The knowledge that security services currently on the market *are* able to identify or stop risks.
- The fact that the cost of data breaches can be billions and plague corporations for years.

What could Target have done better? **Corporate disclosure**. As a public company, the Board has a fiduciary, and moral, obligation to disclose hacks faster. If you're a public shareholder, don't buy a company's stock until you know their privacy policies. Ask whether the company is as pro-active about protecting their end consumer as they are in making money? The corporations of today have an obligation to defend and protect every consumer.

Yes, within reason, but these material breaches must be prevented ahead of time at all costs, and disclosed when they're not. Even working with a top company like FireEye, Target still missed the warning signs. However, we believe that Target was too concerned about losing shoppers in the busiest time of year. Shouldn't they have worried about losing millions more customers in the future?

Anthem's enormous data breach

Anthem is a managed healthcare company within the Blue Cross Blue Shield (BCBS) umbrella — in fact, it's the largest such company in the BCBS network. So, when it announced a major data breach in January 2015, it's no surprise that hundreds of thousands of policyholders were concerned. [15]

What allowed Anthem to come through the fire with little brand damage when other corporations didn't fare as well in similar circumstances? According to Anthem, the reason is simple: It followed its own protocols, which were planned in case a cybersecurity event occurred.

Anthem originally reported that about 40 million records were compromised in the hack, but final numbers rose as high as around 80 million impacted customers. The compromised information spanned numerous business lines, such as Healthlink, Unicare, Amerigroup, and several Blue Cross Blue Shield plans. Anthem called the attack "very sophisticated," and reported that it compromised records

---

[15] Abelson, Reed, and Matthew Goldstein. "Millions of Anthem Customers Targeted in Cyberattack." *The New York Times*. The New York Times, 04 Feb. 2015. Web. 03 July 2015.

including phone numbers, email addresses, social security numbers, addresses, dates of birth, and names.

Anthem.
BlueCross BlueShield

ATTACK

On February 4, 2015, Anthem, Inc. disclosed that criminal hackers had broken into its servers and potentially stolen over 37.5 million records that contain personally identifiable information from its servers.

The compromised information contained names, birthdays, medical IDs, social security numbers, street addresses, e-mail addresses and employment information, including income data.

IMPACT

Over 80 million people (members, past members, employees) are expected to be affected by the Anthem security breach. Class-action lawsuits have been mounted since Anthem's announcement in February.

Anthem said it doesn't expect the incident to affect its 2015 financial outlook, "primarily as a result of normal contingency planning and preparation."

While the breach may have occurred for weeks before it was discovered, Anthem has been commended for its fast action after discovery. Anthem states that it immediately began work to address security issues that led to the hack, and it contacted the FBI immediately as well.

Anthem, perhaps learning from its predecessors in cyber attack situations, also took consumer-facing steps; these steps are always beneficial to the customer and the brand. Anthem immediately began notifying its policyholders of the issues. Because it can take weeks to determine which records were compromised in any breach, Anthem first sent out a blanket email and hardcopy letter to all policyholders. The letters explained that a breach had occurred and noted that those directly impacted by the breach would be provided with further information.

Anthem also provided its customers with some basic identity theft protection services and offered customers who were impacted by the hack the option of enrolling in further protection on Anthem's dime. The organization continued to update its customers via letters, emails, and notices on its web portal.

In May, only about three months after Anthem first announced the hack, Wedbush Securities conducted a survey regarding consumer perception of insurance companies. The report indicated that 45 percent of individuals polled said that Anthem was a better company than similar insurers. Before the breach, that number was 51 percent, indicating only a slight drop in confidence after the cyber attack.

While its brand seems to be weathering the storm fairly well, Anthem certainly isn't without some woes related to the breach. In fines alone, the company could pay up to $16 billion. That accounts for up to $200 for every breached record.

Lessons from Anthem's data breach include:

- Any organization that houses identifying information is at risk for a cyber attack — not just financial or retail enterprises.
- A pro-active approach to a cyber attack can make a difference in how the brand is impacted over time
- Planning now for a possible future attack prepares an organization to react appropriately.

SONY'S MOVIE-MOTIVATED CYBER THREAT

The Sony Pictures hack is an example not only of a cybercrime, but also cyber terrorism. Unlike the Anthem or Target hacks, the criminals were not looking for a particular revenue stream — they were looking for leverage to hold over the company so they could demand that Sony not release the movie "The Interview." The movie is the fictional story of two reporters who are recruited to assassinate a North Korean leader. A North Korean group took ownership of the hack when it demanded that Sony hold "The Interview" from theaters.

The hackers immediately released torrented files of several unreleased Sony movies. The hackers continued to release information on various websites, including passwords stored by Sony, marketing information, security certificates, employee data, and emails from Sony Pictures accounts. Information leaked over the following days even included actor aliases and phone numbers as well as emails containing private — and possibly embarrassing information — from numerous Sony employees.
In the immediate aftermath of the hack, Sony dealt with numerous issues. Its brand took an enormous hit, particularly as its proprietary information was made

available for any competitor to view. Frightened by the hacker's terror threats, major chains across the country made the decision not to show "The Interview," prompting Sony to delay release — an action that caused more problems for the brand. Americans saw the delay as bowing to outside threats.

In addition to brand woes, Sony continues to deal with internal issues. Employees, who claim they suffered because of the data released about them, have filed suit against the company. Some of the lawsuits have claimed that Sony did not manage its information security appropriately. Overall, the costs of the breach are expected to reach over $100 million for the movie company.

According to reports, Sony's information security team prior to the attack was made up of less than a dozen people. The company has been accused of taking a lackadaisical approach to security, which is illustrated by the fact that passwords were contained in a file named "Usernames&Passwords," making them easy for hackers to find. Investigations into the hack also determined that some sensitive files were not protected by passwords or internal encryption at all.

SONY

In December 2014, the Sony Pictures computer network was compromised, disabling many computers. Later the same week, five of Sony Pictures' movies were leaked, as well as confidential data about 47,000 current and former Sony employees.

On December 16, the hackers issued a warning to moviegoers, threatening to attack anyone who sees *The Interview* during the holidays and urging people to "remember the 11th of September 2001".

IMPACT

Macquarie Research analysts projected Sony would likely take an impairment charge of 10 billion yen ($83 million) related to the incident.

Furthermore, hackers have released a trove of documents that include contracts and marketing plans that could influence competitors' strategies and lead to a loss of trade secrets and IP for Sony.

Lessons from the *Sony* hack include:

- The need for increased and vigilant security for any data housed by a company.
- That employees should not rely solely on their company to protect them and should be mindful of possible security vulnerabilities when saving personal information on company computers, logging into personal accounts on company networks, or sending any information over corporate email accounts.
- That cybercrimes are not always committed for monetary gains, which makes more organizations vulnerable to attacks.

CYBERCRIMES: A GROWING CONCERN FOR ALL INDUSTRIES

While the cyber attacks covered in this chapter are among some of the largest and most reported in the past few years, they are not alone. In 2014, J.P. Morgan Chase reported a hack that impacted 7 million small businesses and as many as 80 million individuals. [16] The National Oceanic and Atmospheric Administration (NOAA) shut down its website services for almost a week in the same year; NOAA said it was for maintenance, but reports are that the issues were related to an attack by Chinese hackers.[17]

Other major cyber attacks in the past two years included a data compromise on the iCloud service, a hack of US Postal service networks, and a breach of Snapchat backup data. A brief look at just some of the recent cyber attacks illustrates that no one is 100 percent safe and no network is out of bounds for cyber criminals.

---

[16] O'Toole, James. "JPMorgan Says Hackers Got Information on 76 Million Customers." *CNNMoney*. Cable News Network, 3 Oct. 2014. Web. 03 July 2015.

[17] Flaherty, Mary Pat, Jason Samenow, and Lisa Rein. "Chinese Hack U.S. Weather Systems, Satellite Network." *Washington Post*. The Washington Post, 12 Nov. 2014. Web. 01 July 2015.

3

THE COMPANIES LEADING CYBERSECURITY: STARTUPS AND PUBLICLY TRADED

"There are only three groups of people in the U.S.: those whose identities have been stolen, those who do not know their identities have been compromised, and the identity thieves."

-Joy Gumz

Angel Kings predicts that the cybersecurity market is going to be worth over $150 billion by 2020, representing a compound annual growth rate of over 10 percent from 2014 through 2019. As web, mobile, and network processes evolve, the cybersecurity market isn't just growing in size — it's also growing in scope.

Organizations are offering more data and services via nontraditional methods such as mobile, increasing risk points for cyber attacks. The amount of data being processed across the globe grows exponentially on a daily basis, and almost no process in sectors such as healthcare, finance, or insurance is conducted without touching the web.

WHAT IS CYBERSECURITY?

Cybersecurity (also "cyber security") refers to the software, hardware, and services that protect networks, computers, and data. Protection may be any destruction, access, or change that is unauthorized by the user or is unintentional. The bulk of what we refer to as cybersecurity concentrates on protecting against cyber threats–hackers, malware, and criminals that would vandalize or appropriate data or networks for illicit use. Other cybersecurity products might protect against outages or disaster scenarios.

WHAT MAKES CYBERSECURITY AN ATTRACTIVE INVESTMENT OPPORTUNITY?

As of early 2015, Angel.co lists 130 cybersecurity startups with an average valuation of $4.7 million. Such startups are attractive to investors for a variety of reasons, not the least of which is a general high potential for IPO and acquisition events for any small company in the industry. A startup with a good idea draws attention from bigger companies, and experts believe the cybersecurity market will continue to be dominated by big players such as Dell.

Another reason cybersecurity startups make good investments is that the best companies tend to scale up quickly. Tech firms in general are experts at building on existing technology; they rarely start from scratch, letting then bring viable products to market in short time spans. Because those products tend to meet an urgent psychological and actual need for users, an apt marketing campaign or integration is often all it takes for good products to find sales success.

Investors in cybersecurity can also be assured of a continued and growing need for these types of products. Startups that show an understanding of the market are likely to be able to navigate future needs to tweak or develop products for continued viability. Cybersecurity startups tend to be launched by individuals with high–level technology degrees, backgrounds with large tech companies or security agencies, and, often, some background in startup management.

WHAT ARE EXAMPLES OF TOP CYBERSECURITY COMPANIES?

Dozens of startups are positioned for strong growth in cybersecurity over the next few years, and new companies hit investment rounds every month. One company poised to thrive is CipherCloud, which we covered in our section on the hottest software startups. Another startup poised for success in the cloud security arena is SkyHigh Networks.

Founder Rajiv Gupta says that part of SkyHigh Networks' success is that it collaborates with larger security companies rather than competing with them. In launching SkyHigh Networks, Gupta and his cofounders looked for the hole in cloud security they could plug. Rather than developing another solution simply to protect cloud networks or data, Gupta and his team addressed the psychological needs of companies directly. Specifically, SkyHigh Networks offers technology that lets companies analyze cloud-based security risks, monitor and manage employee cloud behaviors, and encrypt data stored on the cloud. The company secured $66.5 million in investments over three rounds since 2012.

Other companies to watch in this sector include Shape Security, Palo Alto Networks, Recorded Future, LaunchKey, 405 Labs and CrowdStrike.

WHAT OTHER CATALYSTS WILL PROPER CYBERSECURITY?

Cybersecurity has already taken off, and rapidly evolving technology keeps the floor swept for new startups and success. Growing sophistication among hackers and cyber criminals mean legit operations have to work even harder to keep up, and there's always a new threat or security need to be addressed. Since companies can't cut networks and Internet from their processes, cybersecurity products will continue to be a major need.

Every five years or so, the industry sees a major architectural shift in how businesses and people use computers and technology. Recent shifts have been to cloud and mobile, and experts are expecting future shifts to include genetics, biotech integrations with computers, and increasing virtual environments. Each shift drives a new wave of startup and investing opportunities.

The globalization of economies and businesses also drives cybersecurity. Users are more connected than ever before, but laws, cultures, and infrastructures are not. Businesses that can't rely on global governments to protect virtual assets are willing to pay for services and products that will.

WHAT ARE THE RISKS FOR STARTUPS AND INVESTORS IN CYBERSECURITY?

As strong as the industry is, cybersecurity investments are not without risks. The sheer number of founders running in the industry's direction makes saturation and competition a risk, though a number of the illustrations used throughout our book demonstrate that excellent ideas and execution can triumph in the face of robust competition. Another risk for cybersecurity startups is the possibility of quick obsolescence as technology evolves so rapidly. For angel investors, evaluating the people behind the product can help determine whether founders will be able to adapt to the market when necessary.

SOLID CYBERSECURITY RESOURCES ARE THE BEST INVESTMENT

Cybersecurity should be priority number one for today's publicly traded companies. With a fiduciary and moral duty to protect shareholders, consumers, and employees, we're calling on the Boards of other Fortune 500 companies to act responsibly and defend your networks. In fact, here are publicly listed cybersecurity companies helping to protect against cyber attacks.

THE TOP COMPANIES FIGHTING CYBER CRIMINALS

Several Fortune 500 companies have joined the ranks of the cybersecurity elite; enterprises such as IBM, Cisco, and HP bring their technical experience along with hardware and software resources to the problems of security, but they are not alone. Other publicly listed companies, such as FireEye and Palo Alto Networks, are making a name for themselves in cybersecurity, often after rising from roots as relatively modest startup companies. Here's a look at some of the cybersecurity offerings from public companies of all sizes.

IBM (TICKER: IBM)

IBM offers a suite of security services with emphasis on providing expert consulting and deep analytics that help businesses identify risks and deploy solutions. Backed by a global network of BPO resources, IBM is able to offer high-level security solutions with maintenance costs that are affordable for many organizations — particularly when compared with the large expenses associated with data breaches.

In the past few years, IBM has acquired a number of firms with expertise in the cybersecurity market, including access management vendor Crossideas, cybersecurity specialist Trusteer, and another access management and identity firm, Lighthouse Security Group. IBM announced a planned partnership with AT&T in 2014 to establish next-generation security services. IBM's long client list includes notable names such as Dow, Baylor University, BMW, and Heineken.

- **Trusteer Pinpoint Criminal Detection** helps protect websites against account takeover and fraudulent transactions by combining traditional device IDs, geolocation and transactional modeling, and critical fraud indicators. This information is correlated using big-data technologies to link events across time, users and activities.

- **Security Key Lifecycle** Manager centralizes, simplifies and automates the encryption and key management process to help minimize risk and reduce operational costs

- **InfoSphere Guardium Data Activity Monitor** prevents unauthorized data access, alerts on changes or leaks to help ensure data integrity, automates compliance controls and protects against internal and external threats

- **Firewall management** is designed to reduce the complexity and burden of managing and monitoring firewalls manually. Offers near-continuous monitoring, management and analysis of firewall logs

- **Security Architecture and Program Design** helps you evaluate the effectiveness of your security architecture to better manage evolving cyber threats. We also work with you to design a program to align security practices with business requirements and help reduce risk

IBM's acquisitions, along with legacy expertise and systems, have allowed IBM to develop comprehensive security services including:

- Criminal detection services for websites, which combine critical fraud indicators with transaction modeling and device IDs to help site owners identify and protect against fraudulent activity.

- Data activity monitors to prevent leaks, breaches, and unauthorized access.
- Automated firewall monitoring.
- Program and security architecture design services that let organizations evaluate architectures to discover and address cybersecurity risks.
- Software to automate key management and encryption processes for reduced costs and risks.

CISCO (TICKER: CSCO)

——————— Products/Services Offered ———————

- **Cisco Advanced Malware Protection** provides an efficient process for solving threats by going beyond detection. Offers Point in Time Protection and Retrospective Security together.
- **Cisco Identity Solutions** provide visibility into who and what is connected to your network, automation for simplifying operations and adapting to changing needs, and controls for limiting access to information and resources.
- **Cisco Wireless Security Solutions** provides a comprehensive approach to wireless security, offering enterprises the ability to address the threats of access and eves dropping. This at - a - glance focuses on the external threats that a WLAN will encounter and the mechanisms to detect and mitigate these threats.
- **Cisco Secure Mobility Solutions** provide virtual office solutions with full IP phone, wireless, data, and video services to staff wherever they may be located. Security capabilities include spam protection, data loss prevention, virus defense, and email encryption tracking.

Cisco's cybersecurity product line brings adaptive products to companies who are looking for a comprehensive and consistent approach to security. Cisco's approach is architectural in nature and includes services such as:

- Mobile security solutions that increase efficiency while protecting data and processes on a variety of hardware. Mobile security solutions include defending against viruses, preventing the breach of or loss of data, encrypting and tracking emails, and protecting against spam.

- Identity solutions that let organizations track access to the network, limit access, and automate admin operations.
- Wireless security that focuses on external threats and provides methods to reduce or respond to those threats.
- Malware products that protect against suspicious activity and downloads and detects installations and occurrences of malware on the network.

Like IBM, Cisco has built its cybersecurity expertise in part through acquisitions. Recent acquisitions include malware analysis firm ThreatGrid and network security firm SourceFire. Cisco also purchased Cognitive Science, which dealt with AI applications within the cybersecurity industry. Cisco continues to innovate in the cybersecurity industry, and we expect the company to purchase many privately held startups in the near future.

Cisco will also grow its cybersecurity presence by purchasing one of the top companies like FireEye, Palo Alto Networks, CyberArk, or Fortinet.

HEWLETT-PACKARD (TICKER: HPQ)

Hewlett-Packard has seen less merger and acquisition activity than either IBM or Cisco; it did purchase data security analytics firm ArcSight in 2010, but didn't make many other notable acquisitions in the cybersecurity space in recent years. Even so, HP brings its hardware and software experience to the field in the form of integrated security solutions. Companies that use HP solutions include NASCAR and United.

Some of HP's major cybersecurity solutions include a data-specific protection product called HP Atalla Information Protection and Control. Instead of encrypting or protecting the overall structure where the data resides, HP's solution protects the specific data. Protection is applied as soon as the data is created and it lives with the data. The data can be transferred, but it goes out into the world with its security raincoat on, so to speak.

HP also offers a code analyzer that lets companies implement best practices in coding to increase security within all of its software. The product, called Static Code Analyzer, scans the code and provides an analysis of possible vulnerable points. The software even provides tips and guides for addressing security weaknesses in the code.

As part of the ArcSight purchase, HP gained an analytics and event correlation product. Called ArcSight ESM, the product categorizes as many as 100,000 events each second, analyzing events for potential security threats or oddities. The constant monitor provides instant detection for numerous security threats, letting organizations react immediately to stop an attack or reduce the impact of one. Led by innovative leader, Meg Whitman, HP is at an inflection point; by recently separating their hardware and software divisions, HP should consider acquiring a leader in cybersecurity. By doing so, they'll complement their software division and be able to offer a one-stop shop for small and mid-sized companies who need to protect their networks.

FIREEYE (TICKER: FEYE)

--------- **Products/Services Offered** ---------

- **FireEye Adaptive Defense** is a new approach to cyber security that delivers technology, expertise, and intelligence in a unified, nimble framework. Our state-of-the-art technology protects you with our patented virtual-machine detection (MVX™) engine. Find cyber attacks that bypass signature-based tools and common sandboxes.

- **Malware Analysis** (AX series) products provide a secure environment to test, replay, characterize, and document advanced malicious activities. Malware Analysis shows the cyber attack lifecycle, from the initial exploit and malware execution path to callback destinations and follow-on binary download attempts..

- **FireEye Threat Intelligence** provides intel and analysis to help you understand cyber threats, identify and stop cyber attacks, and reduce the impact of compromise. Automates the detection and prevention of zero day and other advanced cyber attacks with our global threat intelligence ecosystem. Accelerates incident response and reduce the time to investigate and resolve security incidents.

A fairly young company, FireEye went public in September 2013. The company raised $304 million during its initial public offering and has gone on to purchase at least one other cybersecurity firm. FireEye acquired Mandiant in December 2013. Mandiant was a firm providing computer forensic services.

FireEye offers automated malware protection and threat forensics. Its product was able to identify the threat to Target's retail systems before or right at the time of the 2013 holiday breach, however, Target did not act in a timely manner to stop the attack. Other companies that use FireEye include the University of California at Berkeley, Investis, and Finansbank.

Some of FireEye's product offerings include:

- A test environment that lets organizations replay and document malware activities on their networks. The ability to investigate such activity lets organizations manage compliance and investigation needs following an incident, but it also provides technical resources with learning and process improvement opportunities.
- A threat intelligence product that automates detection processes so that advanced cyber attacks are less likely to go unnoticed for long periods of time. The product also provides intelligence and analysis regarding threats.

- A complete defense framework that protects organizations and networks, even against cyber attacks that bypass traditional security protocols.

PALO ALTO NETWORKS (TICKER: PANW)

Products/Services Offered

- The **PA-7050** protects datacenters and high-speed networks with firewall throughput of up to 120 Gbps and, full threat prevention at speeds of up to 100 Gbps. To address the computationally intensive nature of full-stack classification and analysis at speeds of 120 Gbps, more than 400 processors are distributed across networking, security, switch management and logging functions. The result is that the PA-7050 allows you to deploy next-generation security in your datacenters without compromising performance.

- **Panorama** provides you with the ability to manage your distributed network of our firewalls from a centralized location. View of all your firewall traffic; manage all aspects of device configuration; push global policies; and generate reports on traffic patterns or security incidents - all from one central location..

- Palo Alto Networks **Threat Prevention** security service protects against malware delivery through custom-built signatures that are based on content — not hash — to protect against known malware, including variants that haven't been seen in the wild yet. Offers intrusion prevention, SSL decryption, and file blocking to ensure security needs

Since it went public in 2012, Palo Alto Networks has acquired several other security firms, including Cyvera and Morta Security. In July 2012, Palo Alto raised $260.4 million during its initial public offering. The company offers enterprise-level cybersecurity for companies such as BYU and Motorola. Some specific security products offered by Palo Alto include:

- Firewalls and the ability to manage them through a product called Panorama. The product lets organizations manage all firewalls from a single location; technical staff can use the product to view firewall traffic, push enterprise-wide processes, and manage device configuration.
- Threat prevention that protects against malware using content-based signatures that are custom built for the purpose. According to Palo Alto, it even protects against upcoming malware.
- Switch management and data center security, including firewalls that offer a robust throughput of 120 Gbps without compromising security.

CYBERARK (TICKER: CYBR)

Products/Services Offered

- **Privileged Threat Analytics** is an expert system for privileged account security intelligence, providing targeted, immediately actionable threat alerts by identifying previously undetectable malicious privileged user and account activity. The solution applies patent pending analytic technology to a rich set of privileged user and account behavior collected from multiple sources across the network. CyberArk Privileged Threat Analytics then produces highly accurate and immediately actionable intelligence, allowing incident response teams to respond directly to the attack.

- CyberArk **SSH Key Manager** is designed to securely store, rotate and control access to SSH keys to prevent unauthorized access to privileged accounts. SSH Key Manager leverages the Digital Vault infrastructure to ensure that SSH keys are protected with the highest levels of security, including the encryption of keys at rest and in transit, granular access controls and integrations with strong authentication solutions

- CyberArk **Enterprise Password Vault** enables organizations to secure, manage and track the use of privileged credentials whether on premise or in the cloud, across operating systems, databases, applications, hypervisors, network devices and more

Even younger than FireEye or Palo Alto, CyberArk went public in September 2014. It raised $85.8 million in its initial public offering and scored a market capitalization of about 11 times revenue. CyberArk differs from many of the other companies discussed in this chapter because its services are directed toward internal threats rather than those coming from outside the organization. Some of CyberArk's primary security services include:

- SSH Key Manager, which controls access to secure accounts by managing access to SSH keys. The manager integrates authentication solutions with encryption to provide high-level protection to keys at all times.
- Enterprise Password Vault, which lets organizations track access to all internal privileged accounts. The product works across disparate operating systems and in the cloud; it can also be deployed in various environments including applications, databases, and devices.
- A threat analytics product that monitors internal activity on the network and generates an automated response or report when threatening behavior is detected. CyberArk has built patent-pending analytical capabilities into the product, which use both conventional logic and user-based data to create appropriate reporting regarding the activity on each specific network. Immediate reporting of any possible threat from the CyberArk product lets teams respond quickly to mitigate the damage caused by internal breaches.

CyberArk's client list includes companies such as Novartis and Pizza Hut.

THE TOP STARTUPS IN CYBERSECURITY

In 2013, venture capital firms invested in 239 different cybersecurity startups for a total investment of almost $1.4 billion. With an average valuation of about $4.4 million, cybersecurity startups make a good show in the marketplace despite the relative immaturity of the industry as a whole. One of the reasons cybersecurity startups are seeing such success is that the industry is currently ripe for disruption. The need among organizations in every sector—and of every size—is critical, and existing security solutions are not meeting all of those needs. The evidence that new solutions are needed is in the growing number of breaches and the expanding scope of those attacks.

Because cyber criminals are evolving quickly, it takes the mobility and agile nature of startups to keep up. Most startups in the industry begin with a single idea, service, and product, working to bring that product up to par with market requirements. Because of this, startups are able to evolve within their smaller scope faster than large organizations—making the startup the organization that is most likely to plug the gaps in current cybersecurity capabilities.

Here's a look at some of the startups currently working on those gaps.

AUTHY

Products/Services Offered

- Authy designed and built a powerful dashboard with all the basic and advanced features like create infinite applications, add collaborators, setting your SMS, calls and many other options created to help you manage your applications.

- Enable, set and decide what do you want to have in your application to create the best experience for your users and keep them happy.

- Our payments system lets you know exactly what you are using and what you are paying. So you can always know what is your account status up to date.

- Whether you require PCI, HIPPA, FIPS or any other compliance requirements, Authy helps you easily achieve and stay compliant.

- Security policies are an essential part of an scalable and secure Two-Factor Authentication deployment. Authy has a powerful policy engine that allows you to automatically control how your Authentication behaves at it's deepest level.

- Authy uses 256 bit's private keys, which can be rotated instantly on demand. All keys are also fully manageable. You can remotely disable and reset keys all with a push of a button. We also provide remote health checking capabilities that help you keep your organization running 24/7 and your users happy.

Authy's main product was a two-factor authentication that could be used by any website owner or mobile user. The authentication provided protection on applications such as Dropbox, Outlook, Evernote, and Facebook and helped keep the user from falling prey to phishing schemes and other similar attacks. Authy customers could integrate the authentication into their own applications, and Authy also offered protection in a payment environment. In addition to providing security resources, Authy helped customers remain complaint with privacy requirements such as HIPAA or PCI. Authy services clients such as Twitch and Weebly.

Authy, which was an Angel King portfolio company, created security products that were successful enough on the market to attract M&A attention for the company. Twilio purchased Authy in 2015 in a cash and stock deal. We also expect Twilio to go public by 2016.

LOOKOUT

- **Predictive Security** - Lookout's advanced security connects the dots between code, app behavior, and known attackers to stop threats – all in the cloud without impacting your device.

- **Missing Device** - Forget that panicked feeling when you can't find your smartphone. Lookout gives you the control you need to get your lost or stolen device back.

- **Theft Alerts** - Lookout turns your device's features – from the front-facing camera to the lock screen – into defensive countermeasures that make thieves think.

- **Data Backups** - Losing or damaging your device doesn't have to mean losing what's on it. Automatic backups of your contacts, photos, and call history make sure they're always

- **Secure App Stores** - Automatically vet applications to ensure policy compliance before making them available to your organization, as well as mobile apps to keep user safe

Lookout has been through eight investment rounds, securing $282 million from investors such as Accel Partners, Morgan Stanley, and Andreessen Horowitz. Lookout's flagship product is predictive software that helps organizations and individuals stop mobile-based cyber attacks before large-scale harm occurs. The product includes analysis of app behavior, code and known cyber attacks to notify users of potential threats. The app also includes services to protect against physical theft by converting phone applications and features to defense resources.

In addition to security-specific services, Lookout's product enhances data storage and backup on mobile devices, vets downloaded applications to ensure they are compliant with security requirements, and helps users locate or replace lost or stolen phones and mobile devices. The service automatically backs up contacts, call histories, photographs, and other data that is housed on mobile devices. Lookout's client list includes names such as AT&T, Qualcomm, and T-Mobile.

Angel Kings expects Lookout to be a top acquisition target by publicly listed companies like Oracle, Cisco, IBM, HP, Google or Apple.

BLOCKSCORE

- **Customer Identity Verification** - We use many data sources to verify the information your customers provide. We correlate data across credit bureaus, motor vehicle records, address histories, watchlists, and other records in order to provide a superior solution to single-source verification services.

- **Knowledge Based Authentication** - We provide a series of questions to which only your customer knows the answer using information separate from someone's identity. This provides a better, practical solution to photo ID verification because it is difficult to know correct answers to these questions unless you are actually the person.

- **Compliance** - As part of every verification, we instantly scan dozens of government watchlists and red flag lists to protect your business from wanted individuals. We can optionally proactively scan your entire user base every time the list changes and inform you if anything changes.

- **Fraud Alert** - We detect mass fraud and use of false identities across our network. When lists of stolen identities hit the black market, we quickly learn of problematic identities and proactively notify you, limiting your exposure to fraudulent activity.

Like most startups, BlockScore attempts to solve a specific problem in the cybersecurity niche. The company, which provides identity verification applications for online transactions, provides services to companies such as CoinSafe, Vaurum, and snapCard. Through two rounds of investing, BlockScore was able to raise around $2 million in capital.

Blockscore offers:

- Identification and verification of customers and the information they provide to reduce the use of websites and applications by fraudulent entities or for fraudulent purposes. One real-world application of this service is to stop fraudulent credit card transactions.
- Knowledge-based authentication to protect applications and customers better than a password alone can.
- Proactive compliance by scanning watch lists and other government documents during the verification process.
- Mass fraud detection, which is bolstered by data-driven analysis of networks.

SIFT SCIENCE

Products/Services Offered

- **Reduce Chargebacks** - Zero in on investigating orders that matter and make quick, accurate decisions. Using the Sift Science Console, see all of your data in one place, including: Signals identifying suspicious behavior, the ability to filter users by IP address, device fingerprint and more network visualizations so you can see relationships between users and accounts

- **Fraud Detection** - With every new piece of your data, Sift more precisely adapts to your business and helps you stay ahead of ever-changing fraud tactics. Prevent fraud with automated learning on our award-winning platform using advanced data science techniques. Harness the same powerful technologies used by Amazon and Google.

- **Distill Patterns from Data** - We sift through your data for subtle fraudulent behaviors that a rules-based system would miss. Behind the scenes, we automatically build a statistical model with your unique data and patterns found on our network. Harness the power of data-driven decision-making in a single platform.

Used by companies such as Uber, Airbnb, and Match.com, Sift Science's products use machine learning to fight computer fraud. Logic and intelligent programming let the startup's programs teach computers and networks to identify patterns and processes that might indicate fraudulent activity. This allows for immediate threat identification and fraud detection.

The result of Sift Science's product is a reduction in chargebacks and financial exposure for Sift Science clients. According to Sift Science, the logic and analytical approach catches threats that rules-based engines would miss. Sift Science also provides a console, or dashboard, that lets users track behaviors and information in a single location, making it easier to identify suspicious activity while monitoring user and account relationships in real-time. Because Sift Science's product is adaptable, each piece of data that is processed by the system results in better performance and an increased ability to accurately identify system threats.

Sift Science was able to raise $23.6 million in funding over three investment rounds including funding from Y-Combinator, Spark Capital and First Round.

We expect Sift Science to be an acquisition target by Google, IBM, Oracle, Amazon or Cisco. Sift Science could also be acquired by newly public Shopify or an e-commerce platform that depends so heavily on protecting itself from fraud.

BUGCROWD

---------------------------- **Products/Services Offered** ----------------------------

- **Testing:** Researchers test your site and report vulnerabilities to Bugcrowd. During this time, Bugcrowd is validating submissions.
- **Final validations and report:** Bugcrowd finishes validations, and finalizes your assessment report.
- **Finish:** A streamlined report of the valid findings our researchers discovered.

BugCrowd's client list includes companies such as Pinterest, Aruba Networks, and Kheroku. The young company has gone through three investing rounds and raised $7.7 million from investors such as Rally Ventures and Paladin Capital Group.

Instead of working on a specific security solution, BugCrowd approaches the cybersecurity challenge from a human resource perspective. It offers crowd sourced solutions for web-based security testing. Customers gain access to over 13,000 professionals, who work in a crowd-sourced environment to test sites. Testers report issues to BugCrowd, and the company validates all reported items before passing them on to the client via a report of findings.

BugCrowd's solutions let site and business owners leverage high-level professionals and a large-scale workforce to vet security and other site concerns — no matter the size and budget of the organization.

Angel Kings expects BugCrowd to continue to grow and potentially be acquired by a larger company like HP, IBM or integrated into the forensics arm of a company like FireEye.

ANGEL KINGS'
TOP CYBERSECURITY STARTUPS

1. Authy (B2C)

Authy tops the list of cybersecurity startups due in part
to its wide-ranging authentication services and the fact
that it's already been acquired. Angel Kings invested in
Authy of its growth trajectory, and its integration within
websites was unmatched. Authy provides multi-factor
authentication for websites, which allows consumers to
safely login to any website with an extra layer of
protection.

2. Lookout (B2C)

Lookout customizes cyber defense for the mobile market
by using predictive analysis tools to plan for threats
before they become a problem for users. The company
now boasts more than 60 million users, including
organizations such as AT&T and Sprint. Mobile security
is the next frontier for cybersecurity expansion. Lookout
is expanding its product offerings to include more cyber
protection and web applications for consumers.

3. Blockscore (B2B)

In 2014, Blockscore landed $2 million in funding for its identification verification product. Marketed as an anti–fraud and compliance product, Blockscore enters the market at a time when newsworthy hacks have made it obvious that simple password protection is fruitless against modern cyber criminals. While Blockscore is competing with dozens–if not hundreds–of security products, it markets itself as the simple, convenient, and effective option.

4. Sift Science (B2B)

With almost 200 million digital shoppers in the United States alone, e–commerce sites across all niches are seeing growing business. Along with the increasing revenue comes a growing problem: fraud. In 2012, online retailers lost $3.5 billion to fraud, so it's not surprising that companies are cautious about potentially fraudulent orders. The problem is that setting the bar too high for "clean" orders means retailers either deny real orders– and lose out on that profit–or they manually review a high percentage of orders and pay out more than is necessary in labor costs.

All of that information creates a perfect stepping-stone for Sift Science, which provides an automated service to sift through orders more efficiently than most basic e-commerce solutions or manual processes. The product uses a rules and data engine to process every transaction against a databank of known patterns, identifying problems such as fake accounts or fraudulent payments. The results are that companies identify fraud accurately, reduce false positives on fraud detection, and reduce manual reviews.

Founded by Brandon Ballinger and Jason Tan, Sift Science has the perfect team for a cybersecurity startup. Brandon Ballinger came to the startup after time at Google, which is a historical proving ground for young technical entrepreneurs. Jason Tan has experience in a number of technical markets and has invested in multiple successful startups.

The product itself covers all of our evaluation requirements. The product also solves a known problem for e-commerce shops, and does so with the convenience of an automated solution. Because Sift Science can save retailers on both front-end review costs and fraud-related costs-in addition to ensuring that more genuine orders are processed-we don't doubt retailers will be willing to pay for the service. According to LexisNexis, retailers spend as much as 10 cents on the dollar to protect or handle fraud losses, and Sift Science's pricing ranges from free to 2 cents per order.

E-commerce fraud protection services may seem more difficult to brand, and you might not see a bandwagon potential at first. But consider the need to keep up with competition. Eventually, more retailers will have to buy in to the Sift Science product or risk the loss of consumers whose orders have been incorrectly denied.

We also like that Sift Science is integrated within thousands of websites. Once you're able to build consumer dependency, as companies like CloudFlare have, you're on your way to becoming a billion-dollar company.

5. **True Link Financial (B2C)**

True Link Financial offers monitoring and education tools for older adults and caregivers to help seniors avoid fraud and scams. Few cybersecurity companies dared to tackle this niche for the older generation Americans. We are fascinated by the potential here and love the mission.

6. **BugCrowd (B2B)**

Applying crowdsourcing concepts to software security, BugCrowd brings more than 15,000 freelance programmers and IT experts to software testing and reviews. With several levels of service, the company provides penetration testing, glitch sourcing, and vulnerability testing. By delivering its services in a more cost–effective, faster manner than in–house resources, BugCrowd hits home with organizations of all sizes. BugCrowd is growing rapidly as it expands its product offerings from large enterprise companies, to growing startups.

7. **Disconnect.me (B2C)**

Even savvy Internet users today can fall prey to the lack of privacy in the online world–search for something once or view a product, and suddenly Facebook ads are showing you similar items, for example. Disconnect.me help users cut through the invisible web of trackers. Users see what is being tracked and can take advantage of extra layers of protection against identity theft and security issues.

8. Trulioo (B2B)

Trulioo offers identity verification solutions for web and site masters, helping users determine what traffic is from real people and what is from bots. In 2012, Trulioo hired a former Google executive and launched a product that sorted real Facebook accounts from spoof accounts–a move that would have scored high on our people, products, and execution lists.

9. Spotflux (B2C)

At a time when Internet users are growing increasingly worried about tracking and monitoring, Spotflux provides a free tool that keeps ISPs, marketing companies, and even Google from tracking online movements. The tool is an encrypted VPN client, and it routes your traffic and queries through a series of services. The activity masks your IP address so bots can't follow your movements for marketing and other purposes.

10. ZeroFox (B2B)

ZeroFox was started by James C. Foster, Evan Blair, and Rob Francis. Combined, they bring cyber entrepreneurship, investment, technical engineering, and project leadership to the table. Add in Blair's experience with previous startups and multimillion–dollar solutions and Foster's speaker and author background, and the group has everything required to launch a startup, manage a business, and inspire engagement from investors and consumers. Not to mention, the founders have put together an impressive team to help them. The team at ZeroFox has:

- Written books about their industry.
- Spoken on Capitol Hill and at major security conferences about cybersecurity, thus becoming thought leaders.

- Built previous high–level, military–grade technologies.
- Appeared in leading industry publications, including Cyber Defense Magazine and Wired.

The founding group and core team are brandable in their niche, a fact they've continued to take advantage of as their startup sees massive success.

The flagship product for the startup is ZeroFox Enterprise, a risk management platform that addresses a growing need for organizations across the globe: social media security. With social networks taking up a growing piece of the Internet pie, organizations can't avoid interacting with them or on them. As ZeroFox points out, "if your organization has people, social media makes you vulnerable."

Social media is a frustrating problem for many enterprises. Locking down social sites can inhibit workflow for departments such as customer service and marketing. Many companies don't want to block employees from their own personal networks, either–allowing access during break times is an easy perk to offer. The increasing sophistication of phishing scams and other social media frauds means that even individuals well versed in Internet attacks can fall prey, though.

ZeroFox enters this market with what it calls cybersecurity's first social media risk management platform. The company isn't the first to market–other platforms offer defensive security tools for organizations, such as block management. ZeroFox offers a solution that goes beyond other tools, however. The platform uses both technical and behavioral indicators across social platforms to create a proactive approach to security.

Users build a database of what matters to the organization–including people and brands–as well as what should be monitored, such as keywords, accounts, and pages. ZeroFox uses that information, along with the overwhelming data associated with social media, to create user–friendly dashboards and alert systems. Alerts are launched when activity appears to impersonate profiles, violate PCI or HIPAA requirements, or include phishing links, among other warning signs.

11. Signifyd (B2B)

With a number of plugin and API solutions for online retailers, Signifyd helps Internet stores boost and protect sales through fraud prevention. Retailers enter custom rule sets for credit card and other transactions, and Signifyd applies those rules in a real-time data review and automated decision process. The goal is to save businesses millions on chargebacks and incorrect payment denials while catching potential fraudulent transactions on the front end.

12. LaunchKey (B2B)

LaunchKey puts security in the palm of the user's hand by moving authentication processes from centralized servers and password processes to mobile devices. Users can create multilevel authentication, including fingerprint requirements, for software or hardware. The product increases security and convenience and lets users customize authentication requirements.

13. Trustev (B2B)

Trustev is fraud analysis software that reviews real–time transaction data for retailers to ensure purchases are on the up and up. One of the things we like about Trustev is the way it markets its concept. Instead of concentrating solely on the protection factor, which a number of companies already do, Trustev points out that two percent of revenues are lost when fraud software catches real customers inadvertently, and Trustev claims to be better at identifying the real fraudsters than the competition.

14. Synack (B2B)

Take two former NSA employees, give them the problem of enterprise technical security, and they do something surprising. Jay Kaplan and Mark Kuhr of Synack are solving a problem that certainly isn't new, but they are taking a different approach that generates a more convenient and less expensive product for clients.

Synack is another company that applies a crowd worker concept to a space where vendors, contractors, and in-house employees formerly reigned. Synack vets its entire crowd workers to ensure teams are educated, experienced, and possess appropriate skills. It sells security services as a subscription, and clients pay a single monthly fee based on their needs. With a global crowd to pull from, Synack can customize security services for each enterprise without excessive expense. In a crowd environment, chances are there are experts available for every system, platform, and industry challenge.

Our product evaluation checklist asks whether the product solves a solution in a more convenient fashion. Synack's services do away with the need for cumbersome vendor contracts, tedious statements of work, and ongoing budgeting for license fees or per-service fee structures.

We've touched on how Synack's product meets our evaluation requirements, but the people behind the solution are also impressive. Jay Kaplan brought experience from the Department of Defense and NSA; Mark Kuhr's experience includes time at the NSA, and he holds a Ph.D. in computer science. Kuhr has published a number of papers on security and worked on high-level research projects within the industry. The founders were more than entrepreneurs with a sound-good idea: they were established professionals with likely connections in the industry–always a good thing for a startup.

We're not the only ones impressed with Synack's cloud-based service model. The company raised $1.5 million in the Seed phase and $7.5 million in the Series A phase and boasts investor interest from organizations such as Google Ventures and Allegis Capital. Get ready for a future IPO from Synack.

15. Shape Security (B2B)

At a time when cyber attacks are evolving quicker than the ability to prevent them, Shape Security offers a product that eliminates the impact of malware on websites altogether. The technology disables malware capabilities on a site, so it can protect even against new and unknown automated attacks.

* * *

Note:

The majority of our top-ranked cybersecurity startups are "B2B" or "business-to-business" products, instead of "B2C" or "business-to-consumer."

We believe this offers a singular opportunity for startups and investors who would like to invest in the consumer-side cybersecurity. The Angel Kings team expects the consumer-facing cybersecurity products to reach at least 50 percent of the projected cybersecurity marketplace by 2020. With the disproportionate number of startups focused on B2B, startups should begin building more consumer applications to protect the home's "internet of things," mobile (Android and iOS) phones, and privately stored data on the cloud.

THE CONTINUED BATTLE FOR CYBERSECURITY

From small to large—from new to old—cybersecurity companies *are* slowly making headway in the battle against cyber criminals. The growing number of startups in this space is helping to close the gap between criminal and legitimate evolution, especially when they develop a valuable or successful product and are purchased by larger organizations with the monetary resources to expand on the successful product.

Still, cybercrimes continue to grow at an alarming rate, and a growing reliance on technology and web-based culture are creating new areas of risk every day. From online learning to the connection of things like televisions and HVAC systems to the Internet, we are creating new battlegrounds for cyber warfare. While the growth of cybercrimes opens the door for new startups to succeed—and investors to turn a profit—it's important to note that increasing vigilance and innovation is required even to maintain a stalemate in the cybercrime battle. These requirements make investing in the right cybersecurity startup or firm a likely win, as long as the company has an inimitable and marketable product that answers a current security need.

Most Active VC Investors in Cybersecurity

Rank	Investor
1	Intel Capital
2	Accel Partners
3	Kleiner Perkins Caufield & Byers
3	Sequoia Capital
5	Andreessen Horowitz
5	Greylock Partners
7	Bessemer Venture Partners
7	Lightspeed Venture Partners
7	Norwest Venture Partners
10	Google Ventures
10	Khosla Ventures
10	Venrock

Figure 2: *"The most active investor in cybersecurity startups across all stages is Intel Capital, one of two corporate VC firms on the list of top investors overall. A few of its investments include PacketMotion, Onset Technology, PerspecSys, and mFormation. Although the firm is missing from the list of top early-stage investors, it ranks highly on both the mid-stage and late-stage lists."*[18]

---

[18] "Cybersecurity Industry Report – $5.2 Billion Invested Across 807 Deals Over the Past Five Years." *CB Insights Blog*. CB Insights, 08 Sept. 2014. Web. 03 July 2015.

4

THE FUTURE OF CYBERSECURITY AND THE BIGGEST THREATS TO OUR ECONOMY

"If you want to hit a country severely you hit its power and water supplies. Cyber technology can do this without shooting a single bullet."

-Retired Israeli Air Force Major General,
Isaac Ben-Israel

The growing number and sophistication of cyber attacks against individuals, organizations, and the government calls for corporate leadership to prioritize cybersecurity going forward. This means both allocating sufficient resources and capital to protecting networks and data, but also taking time to develop response plans to mitigate damage if a breach occurs. With cyber threat activity reports in the millions every year, it's increasingly likely that organizations will be impacted by an attack.

The average cost of a data breach to a major company in the U.S. is about $12.7 million, and larger breaches such as those that impacted Sony and Target in recent years can drive costs as high as $100 million. Traditional passive security measures and preventative controls are no longer enough to deter sophisticated hackers and cybercriminals, who use complex plans to access networks in what sometimes appears to be a legitimate fashion.

Organizations must evolve their cybersecurity measures to include forensics and network traffic analysis, proactive defense tools, automatic threat response, and detailed event action plans.

CYBERSECURITY CONCERNS THE ENTIRE ORGANIZATION

A group of security auditors recently noted that cybersecurity has migrated from a technical problem to a problem of business. In the past, executive leaders and department heads outside of IT and information systems departments could leave security concerns to the technical staff, but that's no longer the case for any organization that wants to successfully integrate security across all processes and data structures. Today, organizations must bring security concerns to training and management processes as well as develop hardware, connections, and defense protocols that protect data and networks.

THE FUTURE BATTLEGROUNDS OF CYBER WARFARE

CYBERSECURITY TRAINING

Employee, vendor, and consumer education are a security concern on several levels. 77 percent of corporations in the U.S. use online learning in some format, and experts estimate that half of all college courses in the nation will be offered online by 2019.[19] With so many people accessing courses online, which often includes downloading and uploading documents and media files, numerous doors exist for cyber criminals to gain access to corporate or university organizations. In some cases, all the hacker has to do is sign up for low-cost or free education programs to get a legitimate foot in the network's door.

The first cybersecurity front related to education and training is securing these resources. Web portals, online

---

[19] Admin. "Important ELearning Statistics for 2013." *CertifyMe.net*. N.p., 04 Mar. 2013. Web. 01 July 2015. <http://www.certifyme.net/osha-blog/elearning-statistics-2013/>.

learning tools, mobile access points, and logins must meet rigorous security requirements; organizations should not allow resources to exist outside of a maintenance and audit environment. Activity should be logged and monitored, and automation tools put in place to trigger reports when activity levels on the network exceed what are considered normal parameters.

The second front related to training is training employees regarding cybersecurity. Training should occur during onboarding and be continuous throughout an employee's career with an organization. Companies should train staff to use strong security protocols including strong password management, to be cognizant of security threats such as phishing, and to use business technical resources in keeping with policies and procedures. Training should be followed with audit protocols that alert organizations when employees might be abusing the system or making errors that create potential security risks.

HARDWARE CYBERSECURITY

While company networks are moving increasingly away from onsite hardware, new technologies such as drones are increasingly deployed in business, personal, and government endeavors. Drones are used for surveillance and defense measures worldwide, and businesses such as Amazon plan to use drones in the future. A growing number of hobbyists are deploying increasingly complex drones for projects such as air studies and filmmaking. Almost all of these drones have computers on board, which makes them hackable. Hacking business drones could disrupt an organization and its customers; hacking government drones could put national security at risk or even start a war. Drone hacking isn't a "maybe" proposition — the hackers already exist. Some programmers have even developed open source software projects for hacking drones. One project, called Skyjack, lets a user deploy a single drone and use that drone to take over any other drones nearby.

IoT Connections

Almost everything is connected today — even toys might come with wireless capabilities — and that culture of connection is only going to grow in the future. As of 2015, 80 percent of people who use the Internet have a smartphone, which means they are connected all the time. When you carry your smartphone, you are traceable and "hackable." Gartner Research indicates that 89 percent of the time users spend on mobile devices is spent through mobile apps—use of mobile apps opens another possible door for hackers.

Aside from mobile devices, the Internet of Things is creating an explosion of connectivity. Your television, your stereo, your thermostat, your watch, and even your stove might all be connected to the Internet, providing hackers with entry points to home and business networks almost any direction they turn. While controlling your HVAC unit via your mobile device probably won't attract numerous cyber criminals, it is important to realize the security measures for mobile and similar devices aren't as developed as traditional desktop security is. As we move into a future of connectivity, mobile security must work to keep pace with cyber threats.

CYBERSECURITY DEFENSE STRATEGIES

Proactive approaches to cyber defense are a growing requirement for organizations and networks. Passive protections, such as encryptions or passwords, aren't completely effective against cyber threats, as has been shown by recent hacks of both IRS and Target networks, where hackers somehow scored credentials to the system before conducting further hacks. Active defense includes applications that work to identify malicious traffic on the network or entrap potential hacks.

One example of active defense is what is referred to as a honeypot. A honeypot occurs when an organization creates an Internet-based system with the purpose of attracting hackers who mean to penetrate computer systems. The honeypot "traps" the hack and can sometimes help provide information about where the hack is coming from. Another example of proactive defense is called sink holing, which involves a faux command-and-control center that intercepts and reports traffic that could be malicious.

The following page shows the **four key trends** that are poised to become the most important industries for cybersecurity innovation and development. Investors and startup founders should know these trends and capitalize accordingly.

EMPLOYEE TRAINING

- 77% of American Corporations use some form of online learning.
- The US and Europe account for over 70% of the global eLearning industry.
- By 2019, half of all college courses will be taught online.
- Access to mass populations and their parent organizations are at an all time high.

HARDWARE (DRONES)

- Practically all drones have computers and onboard logic, and for the most part are communicating with a control system through a communications channel making them susceptible to a cyber-attack.
- There has been a thriving community of drone hackers already and several open source projects available such as Skyjack which uses your drone to take over the drones around it .

CONNECTED DEVICES

- 89% of mobile media time is spent on mobile apps.
- 80% of internet users now own a smartphone.
- Internet of Things is creating an explosion of connected devices worldwide.
- Mobile security options and computing power remains nascent relative to traditional security functions of desktops and laptops.

ACTIVE DEFENSE

- A honeypot is defined as "a computer system on the Internet that is expressly set up to attract and 'trap' people who attempt to penetrate other people's computer systems.
- Sinkholing is the impersonation of a botnet command-and-control server in order to intercept and receive malicious traffic from its clients.
- Threat intelligence is "consuming information about adversaries, tools or techniques and applying this to incoming data to identify malicious activity.

LEGISLATIVE BODIES SHOULD BECOME MORE INVOLVED

From 2008 to 2012, the number of lobbyists on Capitol Hill speaking on behalf of data or security concerns rose by 197 percent. Organizations want government involvement in legislating security, at least in certain regulated or high-risk industries. And, as security concerns become a growing issue for governments, it's likely that legislatives bodies are going to continue to involve themselves domestically and globally. From industry-specific measures, such as healthcare's HIPAA law, to defense measures, countries are stepping in to protect citizens, information, and infrastructure, and that is going to alter the way cybersecurity is handled in the future.

Organizations will not only have to worry about protecting networks from a growing number of sophisticated criminals; they'll also have to invest in compliance measures.

SECURITY SUCCESS LOOKS DIFFERENT

In the past, security that locked down a few computers or a single network with encryptions and passwords was sufficient, because there were limited entry points. Today, technology isn't held on-site: data is in the clouds, employees interact remotely through email and texting, and work is often off-site. Because networks and organizations look so different today, successful cybersecurity should too. Recent cyber attacks are forcing organizations and Chief Information Officers (CIO) to adopt different tactics.

- **Business, traffic, and data analysis must occur** on an ongoing basis to locate and terminate malicious activity and hacks. This is a big opportunity for startup companies, who are designing automations that can process enormous amounts of data so identification of threats is not delayed.

- **Develop response and recovery plans** for both technical and business resources. The question is no longer if a hack will occur on business networks. Instead, organizations must ask themselves when, how, and how big will and attack be, which means all areas should be prepared to respond quickly and in a manner that best protects the company and consumer.

- **Technical staff must spread efforts** between defense tactics, such as firewall and antivirus tools, and offensive measures that hit back at cybercriminals. Analytics and data forensics have become technical tools as well as business resources.

- **Cybersecurity must be tested** just like any other functionality in the organization, and testing should occur on a regular basis and anytime a change or upgrade is made. The need to test networks in cyber threat scenarios is opening the door for a growing number of security companies that provide security analysis.

CURRENT AND FUTURE CYBERSECURITY THREATS

Throughout this and previous chapters, we've touched on some of the current and growing cybersecurity threats. A growing reliance on computers and connections to handle almost every activity and communication of daily life is opening the door to a growing number of cyber schemes and hacks. Here's a look at some of the areas where cybercrime is likely to grow in the future as well as some areas where we might be making it easy on cyber criminals.

RANSOMWARE AND EXTORTION

Data and networks are valuable, which means hackers can hold them for ransom or use them for blackmail. In fact, cyber criminals have even created software especially for this purpose. A specific type of malware known as ransomware is used to hold a system or data hostage until the hacker's demands are met. Sometimes, the system is locked, where the hacker encrypts files on your computer hard drive and you can no longer access important documents and data. These attacks can be levied at a single user or company by encrypting critical documents, files, or software. They can also be levied at functionality on a website — hackers have blocked functionality on sites, disrupting a range of activity including retail purchases and ability for consumers to access service or government sites.

Ransomware isn't always used in cyber-related blackmail or extortion cases. The hack of Sony Pictures is a good example of this — the cyber criminals stole information from Sony and then used it as leverage to force Sony to give in to demands and not release certain films. While Sony eventually did release the movie, the hackers were able to do a large amount of damage by releasing the sensitive information.

THE INTERNET OF THINGS

We've touched on the dangers of constant connectivity a number of times, but the Internet of Things is worth mentioning again here because of the current and growing concerns it presents. In the name of convenience, individuals and businesses are willing to connect large amounts of data and critical functionalities to the Internet. While security capabilities are growing every day, experts have noted that connections can never be 100 percent secure — even the most locked-down networks inevitably present at least a small window for cybercriminals. But what about apps and networks that aren't locked down? Financial and military networks might take a Fort-Knox approach to security, but your fitness app, which uploads data from your wearable device to your Smartphone, doesn't come with much security at all.

Symantec and other security experts have pointed out the dangers of low-security apps on numerous occasions. You might not care much about protecting data about your latest workout or how many steps you take each day — but how about the information about where you took those steps or where you are located for your morning jog? Cyber criminals can hack these devices to find out where someone is or what his or her daily routines are, and then use that information to plan other crimes, such as robberies.

What about the "smart house" — no longer a concept only seen in science fiction? You can turn on and off lights, manage your thermostat, and set the DVR to capture the latest episode of Game of Thrones — all from your mobile device. According to Slate, every smart device you place in your home or business is another potential door for hackers.

From tea kettles with possible spy chips to networked light bulbs that are fairly insecure and might transmit more data than you really desire, a connected home or business location puts organizations and individuals at greater risk of cyber attacks.

PASSWORD RELIANCE

Despite numerous warnings from security experts about the inefficacy of password protection, many people and organizations still rely on passwords as a primary security measure. The truth is, passwords aren't enough to protect your networks and data from a real hack. Follow enough people on social media, and you know that passwords aren't even enough to protect your accounts from teenagers with a penchant for guessing mom's or big sister's password.

Password efficacy is further reduced by the fact that everyone has the need for so many passwords; it's become common to reuse passwords across platforms or have browsers remember passwords on personal or work computers. Now, hackers only have to breach one network or computer to gain access to a variety of systems. Even adding security questions to validate logins, as many banks and other sites do, doesn't substantially increase security, says Google. Security questions often include answers from data that hackers can gain access to elsewhere — such as mother's maiden names or high school mascots. Even seemingly random answers aren't always hard to guess, say statisticians. Did you know that there's a 19.7 percent likelihood that an English-speaking user is going to name pizza as a favorite food when doing security verification questions?

To combat risks associated with password reliance in the future, organizations will have to rely increasingly on new authentication measures, including biometrics. Users — both individual and corporate — must also learn to develop more secure passwords and change passwords on a regular basis.

DOMESTIC AND INTERNATIONAL WARFARE AND ESPIONAGE

The quote from Isaac Ben-Israel at the beginning of this chapter is a short, but frighteningly apt, illustration of how cyber threats are a concern to both national and personal security. Cyber warfare occurs when an international organization, nation, or entity purporting to act on behalf of a nation attacks another international organization or nation through cyber means. Cyber warfare can take the form of espionage as organizations use hacks to steal state secrets.

Other types of cyber warfare might include denial-of-service attacks or viruses.

When considering cyber warfare, Hollywood has conditioned us to think on a grand scale — someone takes over defense networks, steals passwords, and gains access to nuclear missile launch capability. Certainly not an impossible scenario, it's also not a probable scenario. The effort and risk would deter most, if not all, cyber criminals from this particular scheme. But that doesn't mean cyber warfare can't deal equally harsh blows on a different scale — computers control almost every aspect of infrastructure for developed nations. A cyber attack could disrupt power or water supplies; the effects might include:

- Disrupted economies.
- Absolute panic and population paralysis.
- Disrupted security that encourages or allows other criminal activity to take place.
- Deaths, particularly in locations such as hospitals.
- Disasters due to the meltdown of critical safety infrastructures such as those found in dams or power plants.

The United States is taking steps to defend against cybercrimes on a national level. In 2010, it established the

U.S. Cyber Command, which includes a growing cyber force—a sort of Special Forces for the digital world. [20] The cyber force includes military resources with inimitable skills—such as programming, hacking, and data security—that can be deployed to prevent, answer, and assist with recovery from a cyber warfare attack.

---

[20] "U.S. Cyber Command." *U.S. Strategic Command*. N.p., Mar. 2015. Web. 3 July 2015.

5

Ross' CYBERSECURITY CALL-TO-ACTION

A quick tour of the most recent cyber attacks in the United States alone provides for a frightening landscape. We learn that no one is safe from cybercrime, no network is 100 percent protected, and what we thought kept us safe — such as strong passwords and encryptions — is no longer enough. One mistake, anywhere in a system, or one weak link can lay bare millions of data points and impact millions of individuals.

What we also learn from recent cyber attacks — and by contemplating future risks — is that vigilance is critical to protection. The need for constant and evolving defense against cyber attacks has opened the door for innovation, though, and companies are answering that call. From startups to established firms, organizations are providing tools and resources that let us see the digital future in a positive light despite the risks of growing cybercrimes. Beyond advocating for economic investments in our nation's cyber defenses, we also believe the nation should rise to the occasion and protect our people at all costs.

ROSS' CALL-TO-ACTION TO FIGHT CYBERCRIME:

U.S. CONGRESS AND EXECUTIVE BRANCH:

(1) **Pass economic sanctions** every time our country is attacked by a foreign government or state-sponsored hacker. Money talks. Our government should stand up for the people and implement economic sanctions that have triple weight on the nation that sponsored the cyber attack. For example, if an attack against a Fortune 500 company by Russia costs that company $100 million, create sanctions of at least $300 million dollars driven by executive order if necessary.

(2) **Establish a military tribunal** to prosecute cyber criminals. There's no question we're at war – look no further than the

latest attack on the most confidential information from millions of government works. These cyber criminals wear no uniform, act without regard for our population, and continue to cripple our civil and economic infrastructure.

(3) **Expose cyber criminals' own private and personal data**. Publish their family history, locations, and expose their criminal activity to the world. Let it be known that these egotistical, narcissistic attackers are malignant tumors who should be eradicated.

(4) **Create economic incentives for whistleblowers**. If a corporation is attacked and the company or its board knowingly omits or does not disclose the cyber attack, whistleblowers should be able to profit.

(5) **Give tax breaks to companies that invest capital in cybersecurity**. Whether it was a tax credit for a percentage or company's total cyber spend, or a larger deduction for hardware and software (or both) spent to fight cybercrimes, economic incentives would motivate companies to act proactively, rather than retroactively.

CORPORATIONS:

Corporation should no longer hide from criminals and consumers. Corporations, large and small, should share information, create a community to provide insight into attacks, and invest in cybersecurity companies that can help them battle these cyber criminals.

All companies – large and small – should implement the following to make themselves and their customers, safer from cyber attacks:

(1) **Invest in white hackers** who can try to hack into your company's system. (examples: BugCrowd & Synack) White hackers by definition are cybersecurity experts who can hack your system and tell you exactly how they did it. These white hackers are critical parts of making any network, secure.

(2) **Disclose cyber attacks** within 48 hours of a verified attack, data or privacy breach upon your company. Your company should have a specific page on your website that discloses any cyber breach and recommends action. In the long-term, consumers will respect your candor and appreciate what you're doing to protect their valued privacy.

(3) **Reward managers and employees** who take training courses on cybersecurity and data protection. Instead of

punishing managers for revealing cyber breaches, we need to change our culture to encourage transparency.

(4) **Invest at least 5 to 10%** of your IT budget on both hardware and software solutions for cybersecurity. Both are critical components to preventing attacks. Example: if you spend $100,000 per month on web/IT products and services, you should be willing to spend at least $10,000 per month on cybersecurity.

(5) Invest in cloud and email security by **hiring a Chief Information Officer** (CIO). The investment in one person solely devoted to protecting your company is worth it. A CIO's salary can range from $160,000 to $500,000. This is a small investment for the greater goal of protecting your network's security.

* * * * * * *

INDIVIDUALS:

(1) <u>Only work with companies that protect your privacy</u>, that value your data, and have an open policy of disclosure that explains when and how they have been attacked.

(2) <u>Use Multi-factor authentication (MFA)</u> for logins. Companies like *Authy* exist to help protect you from unlawful access to your email accounts.

(3) <u>Don't ever use the same password.</u> There are many apps that exist to do a random password generator. And store your password offline, not in your emails.

(4) <u>Protect your home network's Wi-Fi.</u> Set up a secure router and password, and do the following:

    a. Login to your router.
    b. Enable MAC filtering.
    c. Enable encryption (WEP or WPA2).
    d. Disable SSID broadcasting.
    e. Change your password every three months.

(5) <u>Invest in cybersecurity</u>. Through newly-created crowd funding and equity funding sites like AngelKings.com, you can find top startups that are battling these cyber criminals. We encourage you to visit AngelKings.com and learn more about how startups are now protecting our nation's greatest threats.

Though we'll never be able to fend off every cyber attack, we can help foster the community of startups and create an environment that offensively and defensively responds to prevent the next big cyber attack. By taking the above measures, we can reduce potential risk from cyber attacks, incentivize employees to be more pro-active, and better protect our American economy. At the end of the day, the American consumer, the families and people who make up the American Dream, matter most.

FINAL THOUGHTS

We can defeat cyber criminals. The "we" includes investors, individuals, the American government and American companies battling cyber attacks every day; but winning this next major World War will require new laws, more venture capital funding and greater transparency from American corporations.

We must act now to build the best cybersecurity programs:

If you're an **investor**, invest in cybersecurity immediately. Make an investment in a cybersecurity startup so you too, could reap the benefits of not only making money, but also knowing you're battling these cyber criminals.

If you're an **individual** who is just curious about cybercrime and cybersecurity, protect yourself, your home, and that important data you're storing on the cloud. Never take your data security for granted, and never shop or buy from a company that isn't transparent about their cybersecurity and privacy policies.

If you're the **government** reading this letter, start passing laws that encourage transparency, that punish cyber criminals, and that reward companies for disclosing cyber attacks, faster.

If you're a **small, mid-size, or large company (Fortune 500)**, invest in cybersecurity products, train your employees and incorporate a "Cyber 360" policy on your website. This "Cyber 360" policy is something we describe on our website, AngelKings.com. At its core, the policy means: investing 5 to 10% of your information technology budget into hardware and software cybersecurity, rewarding employees and managers for discovering cyber breaches with a bonus (not retaliation), spending money on white hackers to audit your systems, and disclosing cyber-attacks within 48 hours to your consumers. This 360 degree approach will not only protect your company from attacks, but it'll encourage consumers to continue buying products and services from your company.

I hope that *Cyber Nation* was an insightful primer for better understanding the cybersecurity landscape. We encourage you to learn more about investing in cybersecurity and the many startups that are fighting the good fight, here: AngelKings.com.

To better protecting America,

Ross D. Blankenship
CEO | Author and Expert on Venture Capital & Cybersecurity
RossBlankenship.com

*To learn about how you can invest in cybersecurity and the top startups in the industry, visit http://AngelKings.com